Excerpts from **THE DAY**

Life is a series of tests for every servant of his share. The one test that would bear its fruits down through the centuries even up to today was the test that came forth from his paternal affection.   chapter 1

* * *

The crowning of a Pharaoh involved a great many religious rites. Part of the coronation ceremony included the phrase, as he addressed the gods, "Let there be terror of me like the terror of thee."   chapter 2

* * *

Abortion was a capital crime. In fact, a woman who secured a miscarriage and even a woman who died of attempting it . . . was impaled (dropped on a sharp stake) for her crime!   chapter 3

* * *

King Zedekiah was forced to watch his sons slain before his very eyes. Then he was blinded so the memory of this horrible scene would never depart from him.   chapter 4

* * *

Everyone who had a heathen wife met with Ezra and a panel of judges at the Water Gate, and separation of their intermarriages was completed after four months of examinations. The year: December, 457 B.C.
          chapter 5

* * *

Circumcision was declared a crime. Women who chose to defy the royal edict by circumcising their sons were punished by the slaughter of their innocent circumcised child whose corpse was hung about its mother's neck.   chapter 7

* * *

Titus decided to impress on the citizens of Jerusalem the severity of Roman punishment. The historian Josephus says that 500 or more Jews were crucified daily.   chapter 8

* * *

At half past six on the evening of April 20, 1889, a baby boy was born in an inn in the small town of Braunau in Bavaria. His name . . . Adolf Hitler. It was a name that was to bring terror and death to millions of European Jews!   chapter 10

* * *

It will take 7 years to burn and destroy weapons of the Russian army and 7 months to bury their dead. So great will be the casualties that it will take all of the people of Israel to help in this great task.   chapter 11

* * *

Antichrist, fearing Israel is becoming too strong, realizes that something must be done to crush Israel so he, Antichrist, can have world dominion.   chapter 12

* * *

For the Jew, the long road of trials and tribulations is about to end. The nightmare of the past is about to become the triumph of tomorrow! The sounds of war will be everywhere as nations gird for the final conflict at Armageddon!   chapter 13

DEDICATION / To the Children of Abraham

From the persecution of the Israelites by Pharaoh up to the current Arab-Israeli conflicts, the Jewish people have suffered for over 4000 years.

It is true that other peoples and other nations have suffered, but their suffering cannot be compared to this people who presently are scattered throughout the world.

It is also true that the Arab people have many justified claims and have suffered many injustices at the hands of some misguided, zealous Israelis...but it is more true that the Jewish people enjoy God's prior claim.

It may be difficult for some to believe that I, an Arab, should have such love for the Jew.

But my Messiah was a Jew and we are commanded by Him to pray for the peace of Jerusalem. In Genesis 22:18 we are told that *"...in thy seed [Israel] shall all the nations of the earth be blessed...."*

The heritage of the Children of Israel begins with Abraham. Indeed, Genesis 17:7-8 declares:

> I will establish my covenant between me and thee and thy seed after thee in their generations for an everlasting covenant...And I will give unto thee, and to thy seed after thee, the land wherein thou art a stranger, all the land of Canaan, for an everlasting possession; and I will be their God.

It is my prayer that as the children of Israel read this book, they might come to know their Messiah and flee to him for safety.

THE DAY ISRAEL DIES!

BY SALEM KIRBAN

Fleming H. Revell Company
Old Tappan, New Jersey

Published by SALEM KIRBAN, Inc., Kent Road, Huntingdon Valley, Penna.
19006. Copyright © 1975 by Salem Kirban. Printed in the United States of
America.
Library of Congress Catalog Card No. 75-18503
ISBN 0-8007-0776-1

ACKNOWLEDGMENTS

To **Dr. Gary G. Cohen,** Professor of Greek and New Testament at Biblical School of Theology, Hatfield, Pa., who carefully checked the final manuscript.

To **Doreen Frick,** who carefully proofread the text.

To **Paul Benedetti,** artist, who designed the front cover.

To **Dick Miller,** artist, for some of the illustrations.

To **Bob Krauss,** artist, who coordinated all artwork.

To **Walter W. Slotilock,** Chapel Hill Litho, for skillfully making all the illustration negatives.

To **Batsch Company** for excellent craftsmanship in setting the type.

To **Dickinson Brothers, Inc.,** for printing with all possible speed and quality.

Scriptures used include the King James Version of the Bible and The New American Standard Bible (ASV) By Permission of the Lockman Foundation.

CONTENTS

Why I Wrote This Book 8

Explanation of Terms Used in This Book 9

1 LAND OF THE TWO RIVERS 13
      Haran ... A Cosmopolitan City ● God's Command
      to Abraham ● A Future Promise ● Life, A Series of
      Tests

2 THE LEEKS AND THE GARLIC 19
      The Crowning of a Pharaoh ● The Prosperity of
      Goshen ● Moses ... His First 40 Years ●
      Moses ... His Second 40 Years ● Moses Demands
      Freedom ● Pharaoh Offers Compromises ● Two
      Roads to Choose ● Trapped at the Red Sea ●
      God's Miracle From the Sky ● The Sin of Impa-
      tience ● The Fear of Giants ● Victory in Sight ●
      The Predictions of Balaam ● The Lesson of 40
      Years

3 THE TERRIBLE TRIUMVERATE THAT
DESTROYS ISRAEL 44
      Assyria A Land of Brutal Power ● High Birth Rate
      Encouraged ● Terror Taught at an Early Age ● The
      Parting of the Ways ● The Northern Kingdom's
      Final King ● Sennacherib's Reign of Terror ●
      Hezekiah Reforms Judah ● The Assyrian Advance
      ● God's Judgment on Assyria ● Mannasseh,
      Cause of Judah's Fall? ● Judah's Bitter End

4 NEBUCHADNEZZAR'S DESTRUCTION OF JERUSALEM 55
      Jeremiah Predicts Jerusalem's Fall ● The Time of
      the Gentiles Begins ● Jeremiah's Final Appeal ●
      70 Years in Babylon ● Jerusalem's Destruction ●
      Jews Deported to Babylon ● Daniel's Health Test
      ● Disturbing Dreams ● Daniel Interprets Dream ●
      A Golden Image Erected ● The Test ● The Fiery
      Furnace ● Daniel Interprets New Dream ●
      Nebuchadnezzar Builds One of the Seven
      Wonders of the World ● The Fall of a King

Titus decided to impress on those in Jerusalem the severity of Roman punishment. In plain view of the citizens, 500 Jews were crucified daily!

5 ENTER THE MEDES AND THE PERSIANS 81

        The Law of the Medes and the Persians ● A Rapid
        Rise . . . A Rapid Fall ● The Success of Cyrus ● A
        Free Trip Home ● Would You Accept The Offer? ●
        Sin in the Camp ● The Confession at Water Gate

6 THE POWER OF ALEXANDER THE GREAT 90

        The Path of Blazing Glory ● To Conquer The
        World ● Persia's Corruption ● Esther as Queen ●
        The Strategy of Esther ● The First Banquet ● The
        Second Banquet ● Victory at Last ● Enter Alex-
        ander ● The Tragedy of Tyre ● March Into
        Jerusalem ● Split Into 4 Kingdoms ● No More
        Worlds to Conquer

7 ANTIOCHUS IV DESECRATES THE ALTAR **109**
      The Rise of Antiochus IV ● Invasion of Egypt ● Attack on Jerusalem ● Obey or Die

8 THE JEWISH STRUGGLE AGAINST ROME **120**
      Pompey the Great Invades Jerusalem ● Sacrilege and Massacre ● Titus, Invader of Jerusalem ● The Rise of Nero ● Titus . . . Destroyer of Jerusalem ● 500 Jews Crucified Daily ● Hadrian . . . Suppressor of the Jews

9 THE UNHOLY CRUSADES **131**
      Crusaders Massacre Arabs ● Arabs Retaliate

10 THE HITLER YEARS **136**
      Hitler's Rise to Power ● Hitler Masters The Big Lie ● Hitler's Systematic Terror Against Jews ● The Greatest Tragedy

11 THE RISE OF ISRAEL'S MOST VICIOUS PERSECUTOR **145**
      Jewish Group Opposes Zionism ● Steps to Subservience ● In Contrast, The Hungry World ● The Threat of Energy ● The Changing of Power ● The Rise of European Supremacy ● The Day Millions Suddenly Disappear ● The Reviving of the Roman Empire ● How Antichrist Comes into Power ● Antichrist Becomes Dictator ● The Treaty Made ● The Treaty Broken

12 THE DAY ISRAEL DIES! **171**
      The Day Temple Sacrifices Cease ● Daniel Foresaw Israel's Persecution ● Antichrist . . . A Personality of Power ● Antichrist . . . Master of Deception ● The Master Plan Begins ● The Temple, Sacred to Jewish History ● The Three Temples ● The Abomination of Desolation ● A Pseudo-Religious Leader Aids Antichrist ● Brings a Dead Man Back to Life ● The Terror Begins ● Today's Marking System, Tomorrow's Control ● The Enforcer ● The Choice: To Bow or to Starve ● Israel's Greatest Humiliation ● The Mark and the Seal ● Antichrist Invades the Temple ● Jerusalem, the Golden ● The Birth of Zionism ● Prepare Now to Shed Your Tears ● The Dawn of Destruction

13 TRAGEDY AND TRIUMPH **214**
      Two Thirds to Die ● The Flight to the Wilderness ● The Urgency of Departure ● Satan Thrown Out of Heaven ● The Rape of Jerusalem ● The Battle of Armageddon ● Millions Die ● Antichrist Meets His Waterloo ● The Day Israel is Judged ● The Nation of Israel is Born!

WHY I WROTE THIS BOOK

It is my firm belief that current events can best be understood in light of past history. And, for that matter, so can future events.

I read some 300 publications a week. Some are airmailed to me from Peking, China and some from the Middle East. I also make a continuing study of the Bible particularly the prophetic books of Ezekiel, Daniel, Zechariah, Matthew and Revelation. The Bible is a roadmap of exactly what will occur in the future. Yet I am amazed that world leaders fail to heed its warning signals.

It is a fact that every fulfilled prophecy in the Bible has been fulfilled literally...so the unfulfilled prophecies will also be fulfilled literally!

To my knowledge there has never been a book written which comprehensively covers the 7 great kingdoms that persecuted Israel:

1. Egypt
2. Assyria
3. Babylon
4. Medo-Persia
5. Greece
6. Rome
7. Revived Roman Empire

The first 6 kingdoms have come and gone. So has the tyranny that they imposed on Israel. The seventh kingdom, the Revived Roman Empire, is yet to rear its ugly head. **And its awesome tyranny on the Jewish people is yet to come!**

It is my personal belief that its cancer is already erupting while the nation of Israel is asleep. On Sunday, May 11th in Brussels, Israel and the European Common Market signed a trade accord. Little did Israeli Foreign Minister Yigal Allon realize the import of his statement which in part said: "This trade agreement will have great political importance...we are sure the day will come when the states of the Middle East will live in peace."

It is true! One day the countries of the Middle East will live in peace. That peace will be masterfully negotiated by a personable, powerful leader who will be head of a 10-nation European Common Market type bloc.

But it will also be true, that when that day does arrive...it will be **THE DAY ISRAEL DIES!** That's why I wrote this book. So the Jewish people, whom I love, may be aware of what will happen...and being aware, may find their Messiah who alone will be their final Deliverer.

Salem Kirban

Huntingdon Valley, Pennsylvania
U.S.A.   July, 1975

Explanation Of Terms Used In This Book

Abomination of Desolation

A desecration of the temple of Israel by Antichrist. His final attempt to force the Jews to worship him (Matthew 24:15; 2 Thessalonians 2:3,4; Daniel 9:27).

Antichrist

A name taken from I and 2 John. In Daniel he is referred to as the little horn and the vile person; In 2 Thessalonians as the Son of Perdition; and in Revelation as the Beast out of the sea.

Satan so completely possesses the man as to amount almost to an incarnation. Scriptures appear to indicate that he, like Judas Iscariot, will become indwelt by Satan.

Antichrist will oppose Christ, the saints, and the Jews. He will be first hailed as a Man of Peace and given unlimited power by the European countries, the United States and Israel. At his rise, Antichrist will be only a man, but with satanic power. His sudden, sensational rise as the saviour of a world threatened by destruction will be one of the marks of the beginning of the Time of the End.

His later attempt to annihilate the Jews will bring about his defeat at Jerusalem by the return of Christ. All prophecy up to the return of Christ at Armageddon will be fulfilled by the close of his day.

The False Prophet

Antichrist will be the political ruler who will work the works of Satan. **The False Prophet** will be the religious ruler who will undergrid the work of the **Antichrist.** Both get their power from Satan. (Revelation 13:11-18; 16:13; 19:20)

The False Prophet never will attempt to promote himself. He will never become an object of worship. He will do the work of a prophet in that he directs attention away from himself to one who he says has the right to be worshipped (the Antichrist).

The False Prophet will imitate many miracles of God. He will cause fire to come down from heaven copying the miracles of Elijah in order to convince the nation

Israel that he (The False Prophet) is the Elijah whom Malachi promised was yet to come (Malachi 4:5-6)! Having achieved this deception the False Prophet will declare that since this miracle (bringing fire from heaven) shows that he is Elijah...then, therefore, the Antichrist is truly Christ and should be worshipped.

He will also build a statue, and through some satanic miracle cause this statue (image) to talk and somehow come to life. When the people see this miracle they will fall down and worship the Antichrist believing him to be a Christ.

Mark of the Beast

During the second half of the seven year Tribulation Period, the Antichrist (who previously was setting himself up as a Man of Peace) will suddenly move against the Jews and all those who have accepted Christ as Saviour during the first 3 1/2 years of this Period. In Revelation 13:16, 17 we read that "...he (False Prophet) causeth all, both small and great, rich and poor, free and bond, to receive some mark in their right hand, or in their foreheads: And that no man might buy or sell, save he that had the mark..."

Therefore those who refuse to submit to the authority of this system by having this mark (the Mark of the Beast), either starve to death slowly, or else are slain by the representatives of the government, who will treat as traitors all who refuse to accept this identifying mark.

Rapture

This refers to the time, prior to the start of the 7 year Tribulation Period, when believing Christians (both dead and alive) will "in the twinkling of an eye" rise up to meet Christ in the air.

For if we believe that Jesus died and rose again, even so God will bring with Him those who have fallen asleep in Jesus.

For this we say to you by the word of the Lord, that we who are alive, and remain until the coming of the Lord, shall not precede those who have fallen asleep.

For the Lord Himself will descend from heaven with a shout, with the voice of the archangel, and with the trumpet of God; and the dead in Christ shall rise first.

Then we who are alive and remain shall be caught up together with them in the clouds to meet the Lord in the air, and thus we shall always be with the Lord. *(I Thessalonians 4:14-17),*

The Saints

Those who accept Christ (in their heart) as both personal Saviour and Lord.

Truly, truly, I say to you, he who hears My word, and believes Him who sent Me, has eternal life, and does not come into judgment, but has passed out of death into life. (John 5:24).

For the wages of sin is death, but the free gift of God is eternal life in Christ Jesus our Lord. (Romans 6:23).

For by grace you have been saved through faith; and that not of yourselves, it is the gift of God; not as a result of works, that no one should boast. (Ephesians 2:8,9).

Blessed be the God and Father of our Lord Jesus Christ, who according to His great mercy has caused us to be born again to a living hope through the resurrection of Jesus Christ from the dead, to obtain an inheritance which is imperishable and undefiled and will not fade away, reserved in heaven for you. (I Peter 1:3,4).

Through the quoting of the above Scripture verses God's Word defines (a) how you can be a saint, (b) the rich promises that will be yours when you accept Christ as your personal Saviour, and (c) your eternal rewards in heaven.

Saved

The term "saved" and "born-again" are used interchangeably. In our terminology, one who is "saved" is one who has accepted Christ as His personal Saviour and is thereby saved from the wrath of God against the sinner and from an eternity in Hell and is assured of an eternity with Christ in Heaven.

In Acts 16:30, 31 we read:

> And after he brought them out, he said, "Sirs, what must I do to be saved? And they said, Believe in the Lord Jesus, and you shall be saved, you and your household.

And the well known verses in John 3:16, 17 tell us:

> For God so loved the world, that He gave His only begotten Son, that whoever believes in Him should not perish, but have eternal life.
>
> For God did not send the Son into the world to judge the world; but that the world should be saved through Him.

For further light on this, read the definition on the previous page on THE SAINTS.

Second Coming of Christ

This is one of the most prominent doctrines in the Bible. In the New Testament alone it is referred to over 300 times. His First Coming was over 1900 years ago when He came on earth to save man from sin. The Second Coming is an event starting at the Rapture and comprehending four phases: **First,** at the Rapture Christ takes the believers out of this world to be with Him (I Thessalonians 4). **Second,** Christ pours out His judgments on the world during the 7 year Tribulation Period. **Third,** Christ at the end of the 7 year Tribulation destroys the Antichrist and his wicked followers at Armageddon (Revelation 19). **Fourth,** Christ sets up His millennial Kingdom prophesied so often in the Old Testament (Revelation 20).

Tribulation

In our reference to the Tribulation Period we mean that period of phenomenal world trial and suffering that occurs during the seven-year reign of Antichrist. Daniel 12:1 tells us, "...there shall be a time of trouble, such as never was since there was a nation."

It is at this time that the Jews (and those who accept Christ as Saviour during this seven-year period) will be severely persecuted through imprisonment, torture and death.[1]

---

[1] Some scholars reserve the title **"Great Tribulation"** (Matthew 24:21), for only the latter half of this seven year period. During this latter half...the troubles of the period will reach their zenith.

1

LAND OF THE TWO RIVERS

The desert was hot. The winds whipped up the burning sand making it almost impossible for the camels to plod ahead.

The year, approximately 2000 B.C.

Forcing their way southeast from what is now north-central Syria the nomads pressed on in their relentless struggle for survival seeking the Land of the Two Rivers — Mesopotamia.

Eventually they came in sight of that great city of Ur of the Chaldees, 550 miles southeast of Haran. One day this was to become a part of the country of Iraq...a country of turmoil.

But for today...it was to be the beginning of a great people.

And for Abraham it all would start in Ur.

Ur, with its vast temples and palaces, was being invaded by wanderers from the North!

The Sumerians, who occupied the land, were not too happy with this influx. The Sumerians clothed themselves in fleece and finely woven wool. The women draped the garment from their left shoulder, the men bound it at the waist and left the upper part of the body bare.

This was the Golden Age. The soil was fertile. Irrigation canals made good use of the inexhaustible water. Business with India and Egypt kept the treasury in the black. Even a system of credit was established by which goods could be purchased with interest rates running as high as 33% annually. Gold and silver were in abundance.

Ur had many gods. Most of the gods lived in temples where the faithful brought their food and their wives. The priests in the temple became the wealthiest and most powerful class in Sumeria.

In marriage, a Sumerian woman was expected to have children. If barren, she could be divorced without further reason; if she desired separation, she could be drowned.

Even in those days women enjoyed the use of cosmetics. They had compacts, vanity cases of filigreed gold shells, used rouge, tweezers, rings and necklaces.

Terah had found peace and prosperity in the great city of Ur. Here his three sons were born: Abram, Nahor and Haran.

But the prosperity of Ur soon started to wane and Terah had a longing to return to his old ancestral homeland. At this time Abram was now married. And so Abram and his wife Sarai joined the family in their trek back to the land of Canaan where they finally again settled temporarily in Haran, Abraham's father's original home (Gen. 11:31).

Haran...A Cosmopolitan City

Haran was a turbulent, colorful, cosmopolitan Canaanite city like a latter-day Rome, Paris or London...it was a city at the crossroads of commerce.

Here were buildings of half a dozen different styles...from opulent gold-sheeted pillars to simple sun-baked brickwork.

Here, too, men and women sang hymns to the moon god and gathered in dark groves for worship of a kind which Terah and his family knew well from Ur.

Abram, one day to become Abraham, had become familiar with the best-known cult centers in Canaan. And at night, perhaps he gazed up through the clear mountain air into the low-hanging sky to ponder his own personal destiny.

Terah and his family had been idolators.

God's Command To Abraham

Although Terah longed to go back to his homeland it was God's directive to Abraham in Genesis 12:1-3 that not only started the family moving but founded the nation of Israel.

God's command was very clear.

> Go forth from your country,
> And from your relatives
> And from your father's house,
> To the land which I will show you.

If Abraham would obey God's command he would share in the promises.

Abraham did obey God and because he did, God promised:

I will show you the land (Genesis 12:1)
I will make you a great nation (12:2)
I will bless you (12:2)
I will make your name great (12:2)
You will be a blessing (12:2)

I will bless those that bless you (12:3)
The one who curses you I will curse (12:3)
In you all the families of the earth shall be blessed (12:3)

To your descendants I will give this land (12:7)

I will make your descendants as the dust of the earth;
so that if anyone can number the dust of the earth,
then your descendants can also be numbered (13:16).

A Future Promise

God has already fulfilled many of the above promises.
God also made another promise which will not be fulfilled until the Millennium:

*To your descendants I have given this land. From
the river of Egypt,*[1] *as far as the great river, the
river Euphrates: the Kenite and the Kenizzite and
the Kadmonite and the Hittite and the Perizzite
and the Rephaim and the Amorite and the
Canaanite and the Girgashite and the Jebusite.*
(Genesis 15:18-21)

Some have estimated this land-grant area to be some
300,000 square miles or more than 2½ times that of the
British Isles. This area covers the famous Fertile Crescent
of the Middle East. This Abrahamic Covenant was further
amplified by God in Ezekiel 47:13 through 48:29.

What was Abraham's reaction to God's command?

Hebrews 11:8 tells us:

By faith Abraham, when he was called, **obeyed**
by going out to a place which he was to receive
for an inheritance; and he went out, **not knowing
where he was going.**

What do you think Abraham's reaction would have been if

---

[1] The Wadi El 'Arish, a brook in northern Sinai, was the ancient
boundary between Canaan and Egypt.

Abraham rose early in the morning, and took bread and a skin of water, and gave them to Hagar...and gave her the boy, and sent her away. And she wandered about in the wilderness of Beersheba.

And the water in the skin was used up, and she left the boy under one of the bushes. Then she went and sat down opposite him, about bowshot away, for she said, "Do not let me see the boy die." And she lifted up her voice and wept.

And God heard the lad crying and said to Hagar, "...do not fear, for God has heard the voice of the lad. Arise, lift up the lad, and hold him by the hand, for I will make a great nation of him."

(Genesis 21:14-18)

he had the ability to look down through the future years of time to see the consequences of his obedience?

His people would be persecuted by Pharaoh, by the Assyrians, by the Babylonians, by the Medes and the Persians, by the Greeks, by the Romans, by Medieval Europe, by current history's Hitler, by the Arabs, by the 10-nation federation and finally by the Antichrist!

I believe, even if Abraham knew all that was ahead... he would still OBEY...as Hebrews says,

not knowing where he was going

and yet knowing that God's promises of redemption were sure and steadfast!

Life...A Series of Tests

Life is a series of tests for every servant of God. Abraham was to have his share.

The one test that would bear its marks down through the centuries even up to today was the test that came forth from his paternal affection.

Abraham had two sons: one, **Ishmael,** because of his unbelief; the other **Isaac,** the fruit of his matured faith.

He paid dearly for Ishmael. From the moment of his conception there was discord in Abraham's home. And even today this discord is the cause that compels a Henry Kissinger to make countless trips from Egypt to Israel trying to seek an avenue of peace.

God had promised to make Ishmael the head of a great nation.

> And God heard the lad [Ishmael] crying; and the angel of God called to Hagar from heaven, and said to her, "What is the matter with you, Hagar? Do not fear, for God has heard the voice of the lad where he is.
>
> Arise, lift up the lad, and hold him by the hand; for I will make a great nation of him."
> (Genesis 21:17-18)

A partial fulfillment of this promise is recognizable now in the Arab lands but a complete fulfillment will occur in the Millennium.

Abraham was to live for 175 years. In those years he experienced many testings including the offering up of his son Isaac.

This final test of obedience caused God to make a promise that would bring the Jew many trials but one day culminate in glorious triumph:

> *...because you...have not withheld your son, your only son,*
>
> *indeed I will greatly bless you,*
> *and I will greatly multiply your seed*
> > *as the stars of the heavens,*
> > *and as the sand which is on the seashore;*
> *and your seed shall possess the gate of their enemies*
>
> *And in your seed [Christ] all the nations of the earth shall be blessed, because you obeyed My voice.*   *(Genesis 22:16-18)*

This promise was further amplified in Hebrews 6:13-14 and 11:12.

"Your seed shall possess the gate of their enemies!"

Quite a promise!

And quite a fulfillment, too!

The long, winding road of the Jew, the chosen race, was to begin. Her enemies would make her seem as grasshoppers in the land of giants. Yet she would strive to possess the gate.

Now, some 4000 years later the search for eternal peace still seems to be an impossible one...an elusive one. The conflicts seem greater...the giants, taller.

But God's challenge remains. The Jew is to obey...and in obeying...not knowing where he is going...God will fulfill His promises.

Some 500 years after Abraham, the first oppression of the Jew was to begin...in Egypt. A Pharaoh would reduce the Hebrews to slavery. Then, years later, a leader, appointed by God, would be raised up to deliver them.

Yet, in their desire for material delights, many would still yearn for those leeks and garlics of Egypt.

2

THE LEEKS and THE GARLIC

Egypt, land of the pyramids and the Nile! Imagine the skill of the Egyptians to bring vast stones some six hundred miles, to raise some of them, weighing many tons, to a height of 500 feet! To accomplish this they paid and fed 100,000 or more slaves who toiled for 20 years. This occurred 2700 BC, 13 centuries before Moses!

On one pyramid was recorded the quantity of radishes, garlic and onions consumed by the workmen. And it was for these spicy delicacies that one day the enslaved Israelites would again yearn.

Then the Hyksos invaded Egypt somewhere between 1900-1700 B.C. These were Asiatic "shepherd kings," and not true Egyptians. At this time the Israelite slaves began to build the cities Pithom and Ramses in northern Egypt (Exodus 1:11). At about 1580 BC the Egyptians drove out the invaders and began what was to be called the New Kingdom of Egypt, starting with Amose I and the 18th dynasty. Amose I is often thought to be the new king "who knew not Joseph" (Exodus 1:8).

45 years after Amose I died Thutmose III arose. Thutmose III (1483 — 1450 B.C), called, the "Pharaoh of the Oppression," used the Jews as slaves possibly to help in the continuous building of the temples of Karnak.[1] Pharaoh after Pharaoh took part in building this monumental city until it grew to sixty acres of the finest architecture known to man. It contained a special court, one-third of a mile on each side, in which were placed some 86,000 statues!

---

[1] Some scholars have held that Ramses II (1301 - 1234 BC) was the Pharaoh of the Oppression, while the famed Albright suggested that it was Seti I (1317 - 1301 BC).

Twenty-six of these statues were of Queen Hatshepsut (1501 — 1479 B.C.) She placed this proud message at the site:

> ...You who after long years shall see these monuments, who shall speak of what I have done, you will say, "We do not know, we do not know how they can have made a whole mountain of gold."

> To guild them I have given gold measured by the bushel as though it were sacks of grain...for I knew that Karnak is the celestial horizon of the earth.

What does the title "Pharaoh" mean?

The title is derived from the Egyptian *per aa,* which simply meant "great house," and was one of the ways of referring to the royal palace. The God-inspired writers of Scripture used the term "Pharaoh" to refer to any reigning king of Egypt.

The line of Pharaoh's was passed on to the Pharaoh's eldest son by his principal queen. If the principal queen (or great wife) failed to provide a son, the child of a secondary wife could become the crown prince.

Sometimes the inheritance went through the female line. Because of the belief that the blood of royalty should not be diluted, the new Pharaoh often took as his great wife his half sister or even his own sister. And, occasionally, if no one else was eligible, the Pharaoh married his own daughter!

The Crowning of A Pharaoh

The crowning of a Pharaoh involved a great many religious rites. The King was always known as the Lord of the Two Lands and he had to duplicate his coronation ceremony in the name of both Upper (Southern) and Lower (Northern) Egypt.

During the coronation itself, the king put on many crowns. All the crowns concealed the Pharaoh's hair. Never again would he appear in public with a single strand showing!

Part of his coronation ceremony included the phrase, as he addressed the gods, "Let there be terror of me like the terror of thee...."

It was Queen Hatshepsut who co-ruled with Thutmose

III. She was his stepmother-aunt. Not content to co-rule with such a young king she assumed the Double Crown and Thutmose stayed in the background until she died. When she appeared in public she dressed in the official garb and thus also wore a beard.

It was then that Thutmose III (Pharaoh of the Oppression of the Israelites) began his reign which was to last over 30 years.

From his mummy it is known that he was a small man, about 5 feet, 4 inches tall, with a keen alert face and a large nose characteristic of his family.

One of his first encounters was to go to war against the king of Kadesh and his allies. This war, which Thutmose won, coincidentally took place at Megiddo...site of the coming Battle of Armageddon! In this same pass where in 1918 the British defeated the Turks, Thutmose III, 3396 years before, defeated the Syrians.

Many people think of Egypt as a land of backward people. But even in the day of Israel's oppression, Egyptian engineering was already superior to anything known to the Greeks or Romans, or even to Europe before the Industrial Revolution.

Great canals were constructed, ships of 100 feet in length plied the Nile and Red Sea. There was even a regular postal service (which probably delivered mail quicker than the service today). Credit was highly developed, as was civil and criminal legislation.

Punishment included mutilation by cutting off nose or ears, hand or tongue. Death was by strangling, impaling (dropping on a pointed stake), beheading or burying alive. Criminals of high rank were permitted to kill themselves.

The Pharaoh himself was the supreme court.

The Pharaoh controlled the life of all his subject and slaves. His entourage included:

    a. Barbers who shaved him;
    b. Hairdressers who adjusted the royal cowl and diadem on his head;
    c. Manicurist who cut and polished his nails;
    d. Perfumers who deodorized his body;
    e. Cosmeticians who blackened his eyelids with kohl, and reddened his cheeks and lips with rouge.

The Pharaoh was so pampered that he tended to degenerate.

And it was to such a Pharaoh that the Israelites were in bondage!

Modesty was not a trait of Egyptian leaders. They sometimes adorned their temples with what we would today call obscene pictures and supplied their dead with obscene literature to amuse them in the grave. Premarital morals were free and easy.

Their clothing went from nudity to costly dress. For the most part children in this warm country, till their teens, were naked except for ear-rings and necklaces.

By the time Moses was lifted out of the water, some 300 years after the death of Joseph, the plight of the Israelites had worsened.

The Pharaohs of the new dynasty were not so kind to the people of Israel.

The Prosperity of Goshen

You will recall that Pharaoh had originally given Joseph's family the fertile land of Goshen. This was a pastoral land in Lower (northern) Egypt which lay on the route from Palestine into Egypt.

As the population of the Israelites increased they soon filled all the land of Goshen (See Exodus 1:7).

> ...the sons of Israel were fruitful and increased greatly, and multiplied, and became exceedingly mighty, so that the land was filled with them.

It has been estimated that their population rose to two million people, and the Egyptians grew alarmed.

Thus because of this and other factors the first oppression of the people of Israel began.

> Now a new king arose over Egypt, who did not know Joseph. And he said to his people, "Behold, the people of the sons of Israel are more and mightier than we.

> "Come, let us deal wisely with them, lest they multiply and in the event of war, they also join themselves to those that hate us, and fight against us, and depart from the land."

> *So they appointed taskmasters over them to afflict them with hard labor. And they built for Pharaoh storage cities, Pithom and Raamses.*
>
> *(Exodus 1:8-11)*

Egypt, symbolic of the world system with its principles of greed, cruelty, ambition and force found the people of Israel a threat to their advancement.

The glory that was once Egypt's is now typified by its mummies...dead! Egypt could be described as an illustration of the world. Its temporary pleasures and sovereignty soon turn into a faded glory...a part of the unholy trinity of the world, the flesh and the devil.

Moses...His First 40 Years

Meanwhile, the Lord was grooming Moses for his role in Israel's deliverance. Oddly enough, Moses would be trained right in Pharaoh's court. In today's setting he would be going to the Harvard of Egypt. It was even a greater accomplishment in those days when higher learning was reserved for but the privileged few.

Scriptures tell us in Acts 7:22:

> *Moses was educated in all the learning of the Egyptians, and he was a man of power in words and deeds.*

Josephus writes that Moses was mighty in his achievements for the Egyptians...even in winning for them great victories.

Moses had everything going for him...but God called:

> *By faith Moses, when he had grown up refused to be called the son of Pharaoh's daughter;*
>
> *choosing rather to endure ill-treatment with the people of God, than to enjoy the passing pleasures of sin;*
>
> *considering the reproach of Christ greater riches than the treasures of Egypt; for he was looking to the reward.*
>
> *By faith he left Egypt, not fearing the wrath of the king...*
>
> *(Hebrews 11:24-27)*

His first 40 years in the courts of Pharaoh had come to an end.

At the burning bush God calls Moses to lead His people
out from Pharoah's oppression *(Exodus 3:1-12)*.

Moses...His Second 40 Years

He was to spend **his second 40 years** in the desert of Midian as an ordinary shepherd. Quite a contrast. To many it would be quite a letdown...a disappointment. His training in the university of Egypt had equipped him for work among the upper class. Yet now he was a sheepherder.

Could you make such a transformation? Would you give up a practice of medicine, of law, of education to fall to become a dishwasher or a farmer?

Yet Moses was to get an even greater schooling...an education in the University of the Desert. This training would qualify him to condescend to a nation of slaves and become, with God's help, their deliverer. But first he had to be purified by suffering and humbled by failure! And all of this humbling was to prepare him for **his third 40 years** when for God he would lead Israel out of Egypt and through the wilderness until the Land of Promise was in sight.

Moses...His Third 40 Years

When the time for Moses' leadership was ready...God spoke to him through the miracle of the burning bush.

> Come now, and I will send you to Pharaoh, so that you may bring My people, the sons of Israel, out of Egypt. (Exodus 3:10)

Moses questioned God:

> Who am I, that I should go to Pharaoh, and that I should bring the sons of Israel out of Egypt?

> And God said to Moses, I AM WHO I AM; and He said, Thus you shall say to the sons of Israel, I AM has sent me to you. (Exodus 3:11,14)

When God gives a command for action...God will provide a way. To Moses the way seemed impossible. But our God is a God of impossibilities!

The Israelites at this time knew God only as the "God of Abraham, Isaac and Jacob." They had not witnessed in their lifetime any miracles.

Moses Demands Freedom

Now, under the bondage of Pharaoh, they probably gasped in amazement when Moses and his 83-year old brother

Pharoah mourns the death of his first-born, killed by the Lord at midnight (Exodus 12:29).

Aaron, approached Pharaoh and demanded the release of the Israelites.

Of course, Pharaoh refused. Where else could he get such industrious slave labor free! Some believe that God imposed the 10 plagues on Pharaoh merely in order to convince him to let the Israelites go. But this was not **the entire story.** God arranged the events so that Israel would not only go out of Egypt free, but so that they would be rescued by His powerful arm. Thus in Exodus 4:21 we are told:

> The Lord said to Moses, When you go back to Egypt see that you perform before Pharaoh all the wonders which I have put in your power; but I will harden his heart so that he will not let the people go.

There were three series of three plagues each against Egypt. Each began in the morning (Exodus 7:15; 8:20 and 9:13).

The first series of three plagues had to do with "the springs of life." Water is changed to blood...Egypt is filled with frogs...the Egyptians are contaminated with lice.

The second series of plagues brought swarms of insects, a severe pestilence that infected the Egyptian cattle and finally boils.

The third series of plagues brought hail, locusts and then darkness. Still Pharaoh would not concede.

Finally, God allowed the tenth plague to be imposed on Pharaoh and the Egyptian unbelievers...the firstborn in the land of Egypt would die! (See Exodus 11:4-7)

The tragedy would be so great that

> ...there shall be a great cry in all the land of Egypt, such as there has not been before and such as shall never be again.   (Exodus 11:6)

And this cry would be enough to arouse all the dogs in Egypt yet

> ...against any of the sons of Israel a dog shall not even bark, whether against man or beast, that you may understand how the Lord makes a distinction between Egypt and Israel.   (Exodus 11:7)

God's power and plan were so complete that even the dogs knew who were Israelites and even what cattle belonged to the Israelites!

In this first oppression of the Jews...their salvation from the death angel was to be the shedding of blood and applying that blood to the lintels above their doors.

This was the first Passover for Israel, and it was held in Egypt. Their next Passover was to be in the wilderness (Numbers 9) and their third would finally be observed in Canaan (Joshua 5).[1]

Amenhotep II (ruled 1450 - 1423 BC) was probably the "Pharaoh of the Exodus." He was a physically strong man and boasted that no man could draw his bow. He won great victories in his resubjugation of the Syrian lords.[2]

Pharaoh Offers Compromises

Pharaoh was the shadow of Satan...and, as Satan, he used his cleverness to try and convince the Israelites that there was greater salvation in the temporary pleasures of worldly Egypt.

Pharaoh suggested to Moses that he would allow religious freedom in Egypt and said

>   Go ye, sacrifice to God in the land
>   (Exodus 8:25)

But this was not religious freedom. It was instead religious syncretism—the combining of religions. And it is one of Satan's masterpieces of deception.

God told Moses that His people should take a three-day journey out of Egypt. But the worldly Pharaoh says..."Why travel, stay here in the world and practice your religion. Why be so strict? Modernize your religion. Adapt a new modern message for this new 'now' generation."

This offer was turned down.

So Pharaoh came up with another suggestion. In effect he said, "Go...but don't go far away." See Exodus 8:28.

Pharaoh didn't want to lose a good thing and he wanted the

---

[1]This is the opinion of Keil and Delitzsch, on Josh. 5:10, p. 60.

[2]Some scholars have argued for Merneptah (1234 - 1222 BC), and Albright has suggested Ramses II (1301 - 1234).

Israelities to stay within easy reach of worldly Egypt. But God said, "Go three day's journey."

Then Pharaoh came up with another compromise...he suggested that only the men go.

He realized that if the women and children stayed behind... soon the men would come back...and he would still have his slaves!

When Moses turned down this offer, Pharaoh's finally suggestion was GO, BUT LEAVE YOUR WEALTH. See Exodus 10:24.

This was perhaps Pharaoh's strongest and most tempting offer. How many Christians stumble here...when they have to leave their wealth, their material possessions!

How each of us should recognize the fact that:

> ...where your treasure is, there will your heart be also.
>
> (Matthew 6:21)

Here, however, on this occasion God had determined to give so great a deliverance that even their wealth from Egypt would go with His people.

Moses thus gave this answer to Pharaoh:

> ...our livestock, too, will go with us; not a hoof will be left behind.
>
> (Exodus 10:26)

Pharaoh, realizing that all hope of compromise was lost, threatened to kill Moses if he ever saw his face again.

Two Roads To Choose

The long journey began.

There were two routes that Moses could have taken to the Promised Land. The Mediterranean route could be traveled in about 10 days. This road lead through populated areas. It was rapid and safe.

But this was not the road the Lord directed.

Instead the Israelites were directed southeastward into the Wilderness toward the Red Sea!

Here they would find no highways. They would find no populated cities that would supply their material needs.

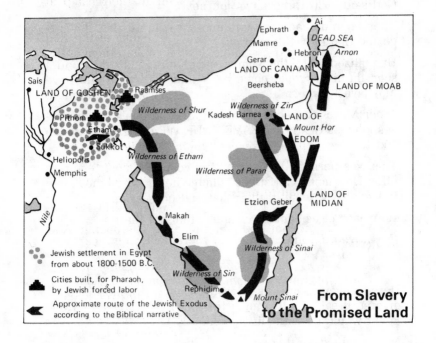

From Slavery to the Promised Land

Jewish settlement in Egypt from about 1800-1500 B.C.

Cities built, for Pharaoh, by Jewish forced labor

Approximate route of the Jewish Exodus according to the Biblical narrative

They would leave the oppression of Egypt to what many would believe would be a greater oppression...that of trying to reach the Promised Land. Two years would be spent in journeying to Mt. Sinai. Then, at reaching the border of Kadesh-barnea, they would be turned back to spend another 38 years in the wilderness.

The Israelites were to learn an important lesson...a lesson that we today could well benefit by. It is this:

> It is seldom that men come to know God
> in their days of prosperity.

> The darker the night, it has been said,
> the brighter the stars.

Israel was to enter into a very dark night!

Trapped at the Red Sea

While the people of Israel were travelling, God provided a cloud. Not only did it protect them from the heat of the sun in the daytime...it served as a camouflage against the Egyptians and it also provided a light to their camp at night in the form of a pillar of fire.

Suddenly they found themselves at the banks of the Red Seas...and there was no bridge or ferry to help them cross.

On their heels came Pharaoh with this 600 chariots.

The Israelities could only see disaster as they cried to Moses:

> *Is it because there were no graves in Egypt that you have taken us away to die in the wilderness? Leave us alone that we may serve the Egyptians. For it would have been better for us to serve the Egyptians than to die in the wilderness.*
>
> *(Exodus 14:11-12)*

But Moses knew that God had a plan for His people. And he commanded them:

> *Do not fear! Stand by and see the salvation of the Lord...for the Egyptians whom you have seen today, you will never see them again forever.*
>
> *The Lord will fight for you while you keep silent.*
>
> *(Exodus 14:13-14)*

What a picture!

The Egyptian chariots bearing down on the Israelites. The deafening roar of wheels and chilling tower of dust and Moses telling his people to stand still and God will do their fighting!

What faith! What courage!

And God did their fighting...parted the Red Sea, and provided a way of escape.

Now two million people had to be fed. Yet they were in the wilderness.

God's Miracle from the Sky

But God provided manna from heaven. The very word "manna," means "what is it?"

And that's exactly what the people of Israel asked.

After the third month of their journey, God called Moses, while in the wilderness of Sinai, up to a mountain where He gave this promise:

Moses, returning from Mt. Sinai, sees the golden calf and warns Israel of God's judgment (Exodus 32:19-28).

...tell the sons of Israel:
You have seen what I did to the Egyptians and
how I bore you on eagles' wings, and brought
you to Myself.

Now, if you will indeed obey My voice and keep
My covenant, then you shall be my special treas-
ure among all the peoples, for all the earth is
Mine;

and you shall be to Me, a kingdom of priests and a
holy nation.

(Exodus 19:3-6)

What a promise to Israel. They were to become a special treasure of God. Their only requisite was that they must "obey My voice."

The Sin of Impatience

It was not long, however, that they were worshipping the golden calf of materialism (Exodus 32). Here were a people who for three months had been redeemed from destruction, had been fed manna from heaven, privileged to drink from a smitten rock...who nevertheless had turned their face away from God towards the sin of lust and pleasure.

And Aaron, who should have known better, came up with lame excuse:

I threw it [the gold] into the fire and out came this
calf.

(Exodus 32:24)

When the people were impatient wondering what happened to Moses [he spent 40 days with God on the mountain] they turned to sin.

Impatience can be the enemy of faith. When Abraham was impatient for God's blessing, he took Hagar as his wife and from this marriage came Ishmael.

This impatience by Abraham has brought tragedy to Israel down through the ages and today is Israel's greatest thorn in the flesh. The Israeli-Arab conflict today has made it necessary to place most of Israel's money into defense and is causing untold pain.

But as to Aaron's golden calf...there is no doubt that there is still an irresistible fascination with idolatry even today.

The Israelites, impatient, spoke against God and Moses for bringing them into the wilderness. Because of this the Lord sent fiery serpents and many died from these bites. Realizing their sin, the people begged Moses to intercede for them. The Lord told Moses to make a fiery serpent and set it on a standard.

And Moses made a bronze serpent and set it on the standard; and it came about, that if a serpent bit any man, when he looked to the bronze serpent, he lived (Numbers 21:5-9).

The pleasures of sin are pleasures...but unfortunately they are only temporary and the payment for these pleasures is severe. The Golden Calf was a form of godliness...and we see such forms of godliness rampant in today's world...but in both ancient and modern instances they deny the power and omnipotence of God Himself!

Charles H. Stevens in his excellent book *The Wilderness Journey* states:

> The children of Israel, in worshiping the calf, had a piety without purity and a pretext without substance. The rankest liberals are great worshipers. Their buildings are often ornate, their robes elegant, and their liturgies beautiful in sequence and impressive to the natural religious instincts of mankind....There is no real virtue in worship. Worship becomes virtuous only when it is exercised in spirit and in truth.

For the sin of the Golden Calf some 3000 men were killed by the sons of Levi.

Accompanying the Israelites out of Egypt were some who were not Jews, but were disgruntled with Egypt. Soon they and many Israelites became dissatisfied with the manna for food. They remembered the succulent meats of Egypt, the delicious fish, the wonderful cucumbers, the melons, the leeks, the onions and the garlic!

And though God had brought them across the Red Sea, preserved them in the desert...all they had to say to Moses was:

> *Our soul is dried away: there is nothing at all beside this manna.*
>
> *(Numbers 11:6)*

"Nothing at all"—What ungratefullness!

This is a picture of today. There are those who desire the benefits and blessings of Christianity, but they do not care for the truth that such a Gospel demands. They want the garments of the Gospel but refuse Christ.

Without the leeks and garlic, they were miserable.

They tried to grind the manna, beat it and boil it...but the more they fooled with it the more it tasted like it was baked with oil. Today, the mixed multitude cannot just take God's

Return of the 12 spies from viewing the Promised Land.

Word and preach it. They must put on a variety program filled with man-made philosophies and false theologies.

The Fear of Giants

Finally, with still other miracles, two years more had lapsed. Here was their hour of opportunity...the time to possess their possessions, the Promised Land.

To go forward would have meant immediate possession.

Over 400 years earlier God had promised Abraham a seed and a land. Now Abraham's seed included some 600,000 fighting men in a population of some 2 million Israelites.

God had told Moses that He would bring them into a land flowing with milk and honey (Exodus 3:8). All they had to do was possess it.

But they hesitated.

It has often been said:

> On the Plains of Hesitation
> Bleach the bones of countless thousands
> Who at the Dawn of Victory,
>   Sat down to wait,
> And waiting, died!

The Israelites could not operate on pure faith. Faith is the evidence of things NOT seen (Hebrews 11:1). And it seems that even Moses needed some positive information concerning the Promised Land. What a tragedy! Are we not as guilty even today?

Twelve spies were chosen for the investigative trip; a spy from each tribe.

For 40 days they spied out the land.

They came back. All twelve of them agreed that yes, they did see a land of milk and honey...

In fact:

> ...they came to the valley of Eshcol and from there
> cut down a branch with a single cluster of grapes;
> and they carried it on a pole between two men...
>   (Numbers 13:23)

This picturesque scene in Numbers is used by Israel today as a trademark on their tourist vehicles.

But ten of the twelve scouts also reported that

> *the people who we saw in it are men of great size
> ...and we became like grasshoppers in our own
> sight, and so we were in their sight.*
> (Numbers 13:32-33)

What, in effect, they were saying was that the God who delivered them from Egypt, who fed them, who provided them water and protection...was not great enough to also fulfil His promise to deliver them safely into Canaan.

Only Caleb and Joshua, the scouts from the tribes of Judah and Ephraim, viewed the Promised Land through the eyes of faith. God told them they owned the Promised Land. But ownership is NOT possession. The Israelites had not yet learned how to **possess their possessions.**

And many Christians, today, who depend on material wealth for security, who worry themselves through every problem, have also yet to learn this lesson of **complete** faith.

Through their continued refusal to accept their Messiah, the Jewish people as a nation today continue to suffer at the hands of evil men until they finally learn to fully possess their possessions!

Because of this lack of faith in the wilderness:

1) All those over 20 years of age were doomed to die during the wilderness period;

2) These were doomed to wonder 38 years, waiting to die;

3) Canaan was lost to that generation including Moses.

At Kadesh-barnea...Israel failed to advance. And that failure cost them 38 more years of wandering. Doesn't every Christian at some point in his life stand at the crossroads of a Kadesh-barnea? What about you?

Victory in Sight

Near the end of their wilderness journey, at what is now the area of the Gulf of Akaba, the people of Israel were plagued by poisonous snakes.

Many died.

The people, realizing they had sinned against God through

their years of murmuring and complaining, appealed to Moses.

Moses, under God's direction, made a bronze replica of a fiery snake. Anyone who was bitten, had but to look at this emblem on a pole to be saved.

In John 3:14-15 this lesson is clearly explained:

> ...as Moses lifted up the serpent in the wilderness, even so must the Son of Man be lifted up; that whosoever believes in Him should not perish, but have eternal life.

Finally, the people of Israel came to their last obstacle between them and the Promised Land. They were at the border of Moab [an area known now as Jordan].

The Predictions of Balaam

This land was ruled by Balak. He tried to prevent Israel's advance by hiring Balaam, a Gentile prophet to curse them (Numbers 22:1-6).

Balak built altars at three different sites for this purpose, but each attempt failed.

Balak was a king of Moab during the time of Moses. He hired Balaam, who was a diviner from the Euphrates, to pronounce a curse on the Israelites. See Numbers 22-24.

Balak urged Balaam to curse the Israelites after they pitched their tents in the plains of Moab. Balaam was promised a handsome reward.

Balaam was eventually to perish at the hand of Israel.

Balaam wanted to serve two masters. He recognized God's divine authority yet he hoped to change God's plan. Balaam really wanted two religions so he could taste the benefits of both...the eternal promises of God and the worldly pleasures of Satan. In effect, he wanted to be everyone's friend. As one writer said, "He wanted to live like the devil and die like a saint."

Balaam was important in Israel's history because he uttered four prophecies concerning Israel. Much of what he said still awaits fulfillment!

A donkey speaks! Balaam, on the way to meet the leaders of Moab, is diverted by his donkey. The donkey, seeing the angel of the Lord with a drawn sword, refuses to proceed. Balaam angrily strikes his donkey threatening to kill him. The donkey, to the amazement of Balaam, speaks saying: *"What have I done to you, that you have struck me these three times?"* Balaam then sees the angel and realizes that his donkey saved his life. See Numbers 22:21-41. It is at this point that Balaam decides to speak only what God directs him to say. On the top of Mt. Peor in Moab, Balaam declared, through the Spirit of God, that not only would God bless Israel, but that he who blessed her would be blessed and he who cursed her would be cursed. See Numbers 24:9.

Later, in a reversal, Balaam was successful in encouraging the Israelites to turn to idolatry. In the judgment that followed, no fewer than 24,000 Israelites perished. See Numbers 31.

Prophecy No. 1

Israel shall be a separate nation

> Behold, a people who dwells apart,
> And shall not be reckoned among the nations.
> Who can count the dust of Jacob,
> Or number the fourth part of Israel?
> (Numbers 23:9-10)

Prophecy No. 2

Israel's claim shall be justified

> God is not a man, that He should lie,
> Nor a son of man, that He should repent;
> Has He said, and will He not do it?
> Or has He spoken, and will He not make it good?
>
> Behold, a people rises like a lioness,
> And as a lion it lifts itself;
> It shall not lie down until it devours the prey,
> And drinks the blood of the slain.
> (Numbers 23:19,24)

Prophecy No. 3

Israel will be victorious

> Water shall flow from his [Israel's] buckets,
> And his seed shall be by many waters ..
> And his kingdom shall be exalted...
> God shall devour the nations who are his adversaries,
> And shall crush their bones in pieces,
> And shatter them with his arrows...
> Blessed is everyone who blesses you,
> And cursed is everyone who curses you.
> (Numbers 24:7-8)

Prophecy No. 4

Israel will be exalted

> A star shall come forth from Jacob,
> And a scepter shall rise from Israel,
> And shall crush through the forehead of Moab,
> And tear down all the sons of Sheth.
> (Numbers 24:17)

The first three prophecies relate to the nation Israel. The last prophecy relates to a person. The Jews recognize this prophecy as referring to their King Messiah...the scepter rising from Israel.

Pharaoh was a hard taskmaster using slaves to accomplish his ambitions.

The Lesson of 40 Years

What was the lesson the people of Israel were to learn from their 40 years of wandering in the wilderness?

It can best be conveyed through Deuteronomy 8:1,2,5,11 which in part tells God's chosen people the following:

1. Obey

All the commandments that I am commanding you today you shall be careful to do, that you may live and multiply, and go in and possess the land.

2. Remember

...remember all the way which the Lord your God has led you in the wilderness these 40 years, that He might humble you, testing you, to know what was in your heart, whether you would keep His commandments or not.

3. Consider

...you are to know in your heart that the Lord your God was disciplining you just as a man disciplines his son.

4. Beware

Beware lest you forget the Lord your God by not keeping His commandments and His ordinances and His statutes which I am commanding you.

Moses was not to see the Promised Land, although he pleaded with the Lord three times for a reversal of His decree.

Had the people of Israel, upon reaching the Promised Land, learned the lesson of the leeks and the garlics?

No.

Ahead lie greater testings, greater trials, greater disappointments. They would be placed in a refiner's fire.

As for Moses...though he could not possess this early Canaan, he would share in greater glories in the eternal Promised Land of God.

Today Israel still seeks her Canaan. Someday, Scriptures tell us, she will find it!

3

THE TERRIBLE TRIUMVERATE THAT DESTROYS ISRAEL

Some 700 years after the Israelites had fled Egypt and settled in the Promised Land they were to face another crisis.

This time the northern two-thirds nation of Israel would be destroyed as a nation and dispersed throughout the world.

And that dispersion would continue even till today.

How did this scattering of the Jew come about?

Three Assyrian kings were to become the moving force behind Israel's destruction as a united nation:

Shalmaneser V	(727-722 BC)
Sargon II	(722-705 BC)
Sennacherib	(705-681 BC)

The first two kings would reign terror upon the 10 tribes of the North while Sennacherib would oppress the 2 tribes of the South.

Assyria a Land of Brutal Power

Assyria was a land threatened on every side by the Babylonians, by the Egyptians, and by the Sumerians. The god Ashur was worshipped and thus finally came down the name, Assyria. The two giants, Assyria and Babylon, engaged in many battles for power with Assyria generally emerging as the stronger of the two.

Their history is one of kings and slaves, wars and conquests, bloody victories and sudden defeats.

One Assyrian king, Ashurbanipal, gazed at the severed head of a conquered Elamite king, as he feasted with his queen in the palace garden. He had the head raised on a pole in the midst of his guests and later fixed over the gate at Nineveh. To another unfortunate general, the Assyrian king had him bled like a lamb, then cut his brother's throat and divided his body into pieces, which were distributed over the country as souvenirs.

Such was the brutality of the Assyrians. And this brutality was to be inflicted on the people of Israel.

The Assyrian army was powerful. Metal-working had grown to a degree that it was used to protect the warrior. They wore copper or iron helmets, carried enormous shields, and wore a leather skirt covered with metal scales.

They used battering rams, arrows, lances, clubs, slings, and battle-axes. Whenever a city was captured it was usually plundered and burnt to the ground and the trees were killed. Soldiers were rewarded for every severed head they brought in from the battle. One can imagine the gruesome scene!

Prisoners were methodically killed after the battle. Forced to kneel with their backs to their captors, their heads were either beaten in by clubs or cut off. Scribes stood by to count the number of prisoners each soldier killed...so he could receive a reward according to his battle successes.

The more important prisoners were given special treatment. Their ears, noses, hands and feet were sliced off and then they were thrown from high towers. Sometimes members of their families were also beheaded or roasted alive over a slow fire!

There is no doubt that the government of Assyria was geared for war. They found it more profitable then peace.

High Birth Rate Encouraged

Like most military states even today, Assyria encouraged a high birth rate both by its moral code and by its laws.

Abortion was a capital crime. In fact, a woman who secured a miscarriage and even a woman who died of attempting it ...was impaled (dropped on a sharp stake) for her crime!

Terror Taught at Early Age

Assyrian fathers, in order to teach their children the ways of war, thought nothing of torturing captives in front of them. They even blinded captive children before the eyes of their parents, and roasted captive fathers alive. To the Assyrian these atrocites were a form of religious honor to their gods.

Ashurbanipal, an Assyrian king, laughs at the sight of the severed head of a conquered Elamite king, as he feasts with his queen in the palace garden.

Ashurbanipal, a king of Assyria, boasted:

> I burned 3000 captives with fire. I left not a single one among them alive to serve as a hostage...By accomplishing these deeds I have rejoiced the heart of the great gods...The monuments which I erect are made of human corpses from which I have cut the head and limbs....

Ashur was the national god of Assyria. He was a solar god, warlike, merciless to his enemies, and one that took divine pleasure, so the Assyrians believed, in the execution of prisoners.

The Parting of the Ways

The 12 tribes of Israel remained together all the way down to the reign of Solomon. Perhaps because the tribe of Judah had been the largest tribe and had been honored with the lead position as the tribes moved through their wilderness journey, jealousy among the tribes emerged.

Down through the years this cleavage grew until after the death of Solomon the 12 tribes separated.

Ten tribes constituted the Northern "House of Israel" and two tribes, Judah and Benjamin, became the Southern "House of Judah."

Jeroboam was the first king of the tribes of the North from 931-910 BC. He introduced the people to ungodly worship, erecting gold images of calves at new worship centers. Ahab, king from 874-853 BC brought Baal worship to its height. It was Ahab who was married to the wicked Queen Jezebel.

The Northern Kingdom's Final King

Hoshea became the 20th and last king of Israel before her fall. He was to rule for 9 years (732-724 BC) before finally being imprisoned by the Assyrian king Shalmaneser V.

Hoshea became king by murdering the previous king, Pekah. See 2 Kings 15:30. Why did he murder Pekah? Apparently he was dissatisfied with the way Pekah had fought against Assyria.

It was Tiglath-pileser, the king of Assyria just prior to Shalmaneser V, who generated the final downfall of the northern tribes. When Hoshea came to the throne this

Jeroboam restores the cult of the golden calf, reviving the bull worship of pre-Abrahamic days as Aaron had done.

Assyrian king had virtually annexed the whole kingdom of Israel to the Assyrian empire. He destroyed cities all across Israel and took many Jews captive.

When Hoshea became king, there was little territory left that was Israel's northern kingdom. Assyria had already appropriated most of it, leaving Hoshea with only the hill country west of the Jordan river.

Scripture records in 2 Kings 17:2 that Hoshea "...did evil in the sight of the Lord."

When Tiglath-pileser died in 727 BC, Shalmaneser V took over as king of Assyria.

Hoshea decided to try and free the northern kingdom from the control of Assyria. For years Israel had offered tribute money to Assyria. Suddenly the tribute money was not forthcoming. Hoshea had made an alliance with Egypt thinking that this alliance could withstand the onslaught of the Assyrian army.

He was wrong. Egypt was weak and divided.

Angered by not receiving Israel's tribute money, Shalmaneser V marched on Israel (2 Kings 17:3-6).

Hoshea went out to meet him, now bringing with him his overdue tribute money. But this no longer satisfied the Assyrian monarch. Hoshea was immediately taken captive. Shalmaneser moved in on Samaria, the capital city of the Northern Kingdom (Israel), and placed the city under siege.

Shalmaneser expected Samaria to fall quickly since Hoshea was now his prisoner. But it did not!

It took 3 years of siege before Samaria fell in 722 BC. By this time Sargon II had become king of Assyria. For a century, Israel had withstood the pressure of the Assyrian forces but finally the nation of 10 tribes was annihilated. Sargon II boasted that he exiled 27,290 people from Israel, transformed the country into an Assyrian province and exacted tribute from the survivors.

Sennacherib's Reign of Terror

Sennacherib came to the throne of Assyria in 705 BC, after the death of Shalmaneser V.

He immediately began his conquest of many cities on the coastal plain. In all he attacked 89 cities and 820 villages in his lifetime. He captured 7200 horses, 800,000 sheep and 208,000 prisoners. He conquered Babylon and burned it to the ground and killed nearly every man, woman and child so that mountains of corpses blocked the streets.

With the spoils of his conquests he rebuilt Nineveh, the capital of Assyria located on the Tigris river.

At that time Hezekiah was king of the Southern Kingdom which was known as the House of Judah. Repeatedly Sennacherib threatened the Southern Kingdom.

Hezekiah had taken over as King after Ahaz. It was wicked Ahaz who solicited the protection of Assyria instead of the protection of God. To gain Assyria's questioned support, Ahaz stripped the Temple of all its treasures and most of its costly furnishings and he drained the national treasury (2 Chronicles 28:21; 2 Kings 16:8).

Ahaz also imported the corrupt pagan religious practices of Mesopotamia which included worship of the stars, child sacrifice and sun worship.

Rabshakeh, the Assyrian General, taunts Eliakim and demands that King Hezekiah show his face.

Hezekiah Reforms Judah

Hezekiah, a righteous man, realized that his first step at reform was to open once again the Temple. He removed all the idols. Realizing that the northern tribes of Israel had now been reduced to the status of an Assyrian province, he invited them to join him in the celebration of the Passover in Jerusalem. Many responded.

Hezekiah knew the time would come when wicked Assyria would not be content. It would eventually try to capture Jerusalem. To prepare for this event he constructed a water tunnel that extended 1777 feet through solid rock from the spring of Gihon to the Siloam pool. The city wall was extended to protect this vital source of water.

The Assyrian Advance

As related in Isaiah 36:1-37:8, in the 14th year of Hezekiah's reign, Sennacherib's army made its move and seized the surrounding fortified cities of Judah.

Hezekiah, yet hoping for a peace through pacification of the bully, admitted to Sennacherib that he had been wrong in not seeking an alliance with Assyria and offered to pay tribute.

Hezekiah now began to make the same mistake as his predecessor, King Ahaz.

Sennacherib demanded a tribute of $1,500,000! To gather this amount, King Hezekiah used all the remaining silver stored in the Temple and in the palace treasury. He even stripped off the gold from the Temple doors, and from the doorposts which he had recently overlaid with gold. (2 Kings 18:14-16).

Sennacherib then let his great army pitch camp along the highway as a threat to Hezekiah.

Sennacherib's general taunted the people of Judah and demanded that Hezekiah show his face. But instead the king sent Eliakam, his business manager.

The conversation that ensued is intriguing and was mostly one sided:

Rabshakeh (the Assyrian General)
You say (but they are only empty words), "I have counsel and strength for the war." Now on whom do you rely...Egypt?
If you lean on Egypt, you will find her to be a stick that breaks beneath your weight and pierces your hand. The Egyptian Pharaoh is totally unreliable.

But if you say to me, "We trust in the Lord our God," is it not He whose high places and whose altars Hezekiah has taken away?

Come make a bargain with my master, the king of Assyria, and I will give you 2000 horses. And even with these horses you will not be a threat to even the least lieutenant in charge of the smallest contingent of our army!

The King of Assyria says, "Make your peace with me and come out to me, and eat each of his vine and each of his fig tree and drink each of the waters of his own cistern.

But do not listen to Hezekiah, when he misleads you, saying, The Lord will deliver us."

Has any one of the gods of the nations delivered his land from the hand of the King of Assyria?
(2 Kings 19:20-33)

Eliakim only requested that Rabshakeh speak in Aramaic so the general populace would not hear but he was rebuked.

Then it happened that night that the angel of the Lord went out, and struck 185,000 in the camp of the Assyrians; and when men rose early in the morning, behold, all of them were dead (2 Kings 19:35).

Hezekiah, upon hearing of this encounter was so distraught that he tore his clothes, covered himself with sackcloth and entered the Temple.

Isaiah, the prophet encouraged Hezekiah, told him not to be afraid of the threats the Assyrian general had uttered. Isaiah further said:

> *Behold, I will put a spirit in him [Sennacherib] so that he shall hear a rumor and return to his own land. And I will make him fall by the sword in his own land.* (Isaiah 37:7)

It was shortly after that when Sennacherib received word that Babylon was in rebellion. He thus for the time abandoned his siege without conquering Jerusalem!

Sennacherib finally destroyed Babylon in 689 BC after about 10 years of fighting.

God's Judgment on Assyria

Once again this Assyrian king turned towards Jerusalem and sent a letter to Hezekiah demanding he surrender (2 Kings 19:9).

Hezekiah took the letter to the Temple and prayed, knowing that God would deliver Judah.

From Isaiah came the message that Sennacherib would not be successful in his threat. Isaiah's prophecy included this punishment to Assyria:

> Because of your raging against Me,
> And because your arrogance has come up to My
>   ears,
> Therefore I will put My hook in your nose,
> And My bridle in your lips,
> And I will turn you back by the way which you
>   came.   (2 Kings 19:28)

That night the angel of the Lord killed 185,000 Assyrian troops and dead bodies were seen all across the landscape in the morning.

Then King Sennacherib returned to Nineveh, and as he was worshiping in the temple of his god, his sons killed him, just as had been predicted by Isaiah years earlier! (Isaiah 37:7; 2 Kings 19:37).

Manasseh, Cause of Judah's Fall?

When Hezekiah died, his son Manasseh took over as king of Judah. He was to rule 55 years, 10 years as co-ruler with his father and 45 years alone, the longest of any king in either Judah or Israel.

Manasseh, instead of following his father's example, returned to religious idolatry in the footsteps of his grandfather, Ahaz. He even erected an image of the Canaanite goddess, Asherah, in the Temple. And when anyone protested, he simply killed them.

Some believe Isaiah was among the victims of this period.

Finally God's judgment came down on Manasseh and he was taken captive by an Assyrian king.

Eventually Manasseh was permitted to return to Judah and he sought to make amends for his past wickedness.

Except for the great king, Josiah (ruled 640-609 BC), there were a few minor kings after Manasseh's death.

Judah's Bitter End

The final king, before Judah came under the threat of Nebuchadnezzar, was Jehoiakim (609-597 BC).

A sudden turn in events saw a newly revived Babylon victorious over the Assyrians. The king in Babylon, Nebuchadnezzar, urged his satellite countries to invade Judah.

Jehoiakim was both greedy and unprincipled. He tried to kill Jeremiah and Baruch who prophesied against his ungodly leadership.

Before Nebuchadnezzar reached Jerusalem, Jehoiakim died in 597 BC.

His son, Jehoiachin was to reign only 3 months and 10 days. For in the Spring of 597 BC Jerusalem was captured.

And Judah, the Southern Kingdom of the two tribes, was now to enter into bondage under Nebuchadnezzar. The last puppet King of Judah was Zedekiah (ruled 597-586 BC). He, however, revolted against Nebuchadnezzar. In answer to this Nebuchadnezzar besieged Jerusalem, put out Zedekiah's eyes after slaying his children before him, and tore down the Temple of God built by Solomon. This occurred in 586 BC, and so was Judah destroyed and its holy Temple no more.

The 12 Tribes of Israel were no more a Kingdom. First the 10 Tribes had been dispersed in 721 BC and finally, 135 years later, in 586 BC the southern kingdom of Judah and Benjamin were entirely defeated.

Israel was no more a nation! And, except for the Maccabean (a Jewish family) rule of 165-63 BC, over 2000 years would pass before any form of lasting unity would come. But even today, although there is a nation, Israel, many Jews remain scattered throughout all the world.

Thus, the first two oppressions of Israel had ended...the oppression under Egypt and the oppression under Assyria.

Ahead lie more world empires that would rule over or dominate the people of Israel. These empires of Gentile domination would be the reflected in the prophecies of Daniel in his interpretation of the great statue of Daniel 2:31-45.

4

NEBUCHADNEZZAR'S DESTRUCTION OF JERUSALEM

At 21, Jeremiah realized that God had a special plan for his life. He was not to marry. He was to be a prophet of God.

About 607 B.C., Jeremiah stood in the temple court of Jerusalem and warned the people that if they did not obey God's commandments...the temple would suffer the same fate as Shiloh.

> Shiloh, about 12 miles from Jacob's well, was at one time a very important city. But by Jeremiah's day, because of apostasy, it was in ruins...long since forgotten. The tabernacle of Moses was destroyed by the invading Philistines.

He warned the Jews of their hypocrisy when he questioned:

> Will you steal, murder, and commit adultery, and swear falsely, and offer sacrifices to Baal, and walk after other gods that you have not known, then come and stand before Me in this house, which is called by My name, and say, "We are delivered!" — that you may do all these abominations? (Jeremiah 7:9-10)

In effect, Jeremiah was accusing the Jews of going to the temple to get cleansing from sin and then saying, after the service was over, "We are delivered from past sins...now we are ready to start sinning all over again!"

The leaders, upset by the fact that Jeremiah prophesied that Jerusalem would die...that Jerusalem would become the property of Nebuchadnezzar...charged their audience that

> *This man is worthy to die; for he has prophesied against this city.... (Jeremiah 26:11)*

Judah was guilty of many sins in Jeremiah's day and God, through him, speaks:

> *Roam to and fro through the streets of Jerusalem,*
> *   And look now, and take note.*
> *   And seek in her open square,*
> *   If you can find a man,*
> *   If there is one who does justice, who seeks*
> *   truth,*
> *   Then I will pardon her.*
>
> *   (Jeremiah 5:1)*

God continues to warn them:

> *...a lion from the forest shall slay them,*
> *A wolf of the deserts shall destroy them,*
> *A leopard is watching their cities.*
> *Everyone who goes out of them shall be torn in*
> *   pieces,*
> *Because their transgressions are many,*
> *Their apostasies are numerous.*
>
> *   (Jeremiah 5:6)*

And God, through Jeremiah, asks the question:

> *Why should I pardon you?*
> *Your sons have forsaken Me*
> *And sworn by those who are not gods.*
>
> *When I fed them to the full*
> *They committed adultery*
> *And trooped to the harlot's house.*
>
> *They were well-fed lusty horses,*
> *Each one neighing after his neighbor's wife.*
>
> *Shall I not punish these people, declares the Lord,*
> *And on a nation such as this*
> *Shall I not avenge Myself?*
>
> *   (Jeremiah 5:7-9)*

Jeremiah Predicts Jerusalem's Fall

Then, Jeremiah predicts what will happen to Jerusalem because the people have failed to honor God. These predictions are found in Jeremiah 5:13-19. There were 12 predictions. All were fulfilled with Nebuchadnezzar's invasion of Jerusalem. Here they are:

1. The false prophets will be discovered and their lies will be exposed.

2. Jeremiah's words will be like fire. The people will be as wood. And the prophet's words will condemn them.

3. A nation from afar will invade Jerusalem (Babylon).

4. It will be a mighty nation. (Babylon had already defeated fearless Assyria!)

5. It will be an ancient nation. (Babylon was in existence, possibly since 3000 B.C.) (And at the time of this prediction...it was about 600 B.C.)

6. It will be one whose language you do not know. You won't be able to understand what they are saying. (The formal language of Babylon was Akkadian...but the conversational language was called Aramaic.)

7. Their arrows will mean sure death because they are skillful soldiers.

8. They will eat up your harvest and they will also eat the food meant for your sons and daughters.

9. They will also eat your flocks and your herds.

10. They will eat your grapes and fig trees as well.

11. They will destroy the cities of Judah even though they are protected by walls.

12. You will be serving strangers in a land that is not yours.

In spite of this warning from the prophet Jeremiah...the people went on living in sin and disobeying God.

Nebuchadnezzar forces Zedekiah to watch his sons slain before his very eyes. Then he was blinded so the memory of this horrible scene would never depart from him (Jeremiah 39:6-7).

The Sequence of Events in
NEBUCHADNEZZAR'S DESTRUCTION OF JERUSALEM

The destruction of Jerusalem by Nebuchadnezzar was accomplished in 3 stages:

The First attack   **606-605 B.C.**

Jehoiakim was King over Judah. He was 25. His appointment was made by the king of Egypt who at this time controlled this area. Jehoiakim was an oppressive king and godless. Many of the prophecies of Jeremiah were uttered against this cruel ruler.

When Egypt was overrun by Nebuchadnezzar, the Babylonian king allowed Jehoiakim to remain ruler in Jerusalem. He reigned for 11 years. However, when Jehoiakim became too independent...Nebuchadnezzar captured Jerusalem... took King Jehoiakim to Babylon as his prisoner, and bound him in bronze chains. He also took some of the sacred vessels from the Temple and some select young men... among which was 16-year-old Daniel. Jehoiakim died in disgrace. Nebuchadnezzar then placed Jehoiachin (son of Jehoiakim) on the throne of Judah.

The Second attack   597 B.C.
Jehoiachin, following his father's footsteps...also did evil in the sight of the Lord. See Kings 24:9. His reign in Jerusalem lasted only 3 months. The Babylonian army besieged Jerusalem, finally capturing it on March 15, 597 B.C. Jehoiachin...together with his wives, his mother, and 10,000 of Jerusalem's leading citizens appeared before Nebuchadnezzar to personally hear their judgment from his own lips. The penalty: permanent deportation to Babylon!

A young 25-year-old priest named Ezekiel was among the citizens deported to Babylon. Nebuchadnezzar also took more treasures from the Temple...leaving just enough sacred furniture for religious ceremonies to be carried out under his new puppet king...21-year-old Zedekiah.

The Third attack   587-586 B.C.
The final invasion of Jerusalem started in 587 B.C. Zedekiah was Jehoiachin's uncle. Nebuchadnezzar was not too sure of Zedekiah's loyalty. Apparently Zedekiah wasn't either. For when it became evident that Zedekiah was compromising between loyalty to Babylon and loyalty to Egypt ...Nebuchadnezzar became very angry. For some 30 months Nebuchadnezzar's army lay siege to Jerusalem. Finally, on July 18, 586 B.C., the city walls were breached.

The Temple was destroyed by fire. Jerusalem was burned to the ground. The remainder of the sacred vessels were taken. The survivors, chained like wild animals, were deported to Babylon. Zedekiah was forced to watch his sons slain before his very eyes. Then he was blinded so the memory of this horrible scene would never depart from him (Jeremiah 39:6-7). He was then taken to Babylon where he died. Zedekiah's reign had lasted 11 years.

Judgment Strikes

Then God told Jeremiah:

> You shall speak all these words to them, but they will not listen to you; and you shall call to them, but they will not answer you.
>
> And you shall say to them, This is the nation that did not obey the voice of the Lord their God or accept correction; truth has perished and has been cut off from their mouth.
>
> Therefore...days are coming [when this valley will be called] the valley of the Slaughter...
>
> And the dead bodies of this people will be food for the birds of the sky, and for the beasts of the earth; and no one will frighten them away...the land will become a ruin. (Jeremiah 7:27,28,32-34)

And that day did come to pass.

In the third attack on Jerusalem, Nebuchadnezzar's army encircled the city for 30 months, paralyzing it in a state of siege.

So starved were the people of Jerusalem that many of them finally turned to cannibalism to ease their severe hunger:

> The hands of compassionate women
> Boiled their own children;
> They become food for them...
> (Lamentations 4:10)

This may be difficult to understand. But you must remember that the nation had gone into the depths of idolatry... when they even offered their sons and daughters to the false god, Molech. It was Solomon who built an altar to Molech and this idol worship continued at intervals until Josiah destroyed the altars.

The Babylonian soldiers brutally mistreated the Jews.

> They ravished the women in Zion,
> The virgins in the cities of Judah.
>
> Princes were hung by their hands;
> Aged men are treated with contempt,
>
> They take away the young men to grind their grain
> And the little children stagger beneath their heavy
> loads. (Lamentations 5:11-13)

They then herded them together and chained the Jews like wild animals for deportation to Babylon.

It seems as though history repeats itself...for Hitler, during World War 2, gathered the Jews, tortured and killed them, and deported them to concentration camps.

About a month after Jerusalem was taken, a Babylonian general named Nebuzaradan began the systematic destruction of Jerusalem. He tore down the city walls; he burned to the ground the Temple, the palace and many of the houses.

And what sacred vessels had not been previously taken in the first two attacks on Jerusalem...he shipped to Babylon.

Then, two months after Jerusalem was burned, Gedaliah, the governor of Judah...and a friend of Jeremiah...along with many people, were brutally slain by a traitorous prince named Ishmael.

Israel's initial experience as a divinely-established nation on earth had come to an end.

The Time of The Gentiles Begins

The period of Babylonian captivity had begun. This was the start of the time of the Gentiles and a fulfillment of Hosea 3:4-5:

> For the sons of Israel will remain for many days without a king or prince, without sacrifice or sacred pillar, and without ephod [sacred vestment] or household idols.

> Afterward the sons of Israel will return and seek the Lord their God and David their king; and they will come trembling to the Lord and to His goodness in the last days.

Judah (Israel) was permitted to suffer the horrors of Babylonian captivity for three basic reasons:

1. Zedediah refused God's Word and also broke his oath of loyalty to Nebuchadnezzar.

2. Both the priests and the people adopted heathen customs. They polluted the Temple and ridiculed God's prophets.

3. The people had not honored God's commandment that on the seventh year the land should rest...no crops were to be planted.

Judahites being taken into Babylonian captivity.

Jerusalem suffered deep humiliation and Jeremiah laments:

1. Her gates have sunk into the ground
2. He has destroyed and broken her bars
3. Her kings and princes are [captives] among the nations
4. The law is no more
5. Her prophets find no vision from the Lord
6. The elders sit on the ground
7. They are speechless
8. They have thrown dust on their heads
9. They have girded themselves with sackcloth
10. The virgins of Jerusalem have bowed their heads to the ground [in shame]
11. The people are destroyed
12. The children and babies die of hunger

(Lamentations 2:9-11)

Jeremiah's Final Appeal

In a final cry for mercy Jeremiah pleads:

Remember, O Lord, what has befallen us;

*Our inheritance has been turned over to
strangers,*
Our houses to aliens.
We have become orphans without a father,
Our mothers are like widows.

We have to pay for our drinking water,
Our wood comes to us at a price.

Our pursuers are at our necks;
We are worn out, there is no rest for us.

*We have submitted to Egypt and Assyria to get
enough bread.*
Our fathers have sinned, and are no more;
It is we who have borne their iniquities.

Slaves rule over us;
There is no one to deliver us from their hand.

(Lamentations 5:1-8)

How sad is this day for Israel when Jeremiah in Lamentations 5:16 and 1:1,12 recognizes the fact that

The crown has fallen from our head.

How lonely sits the city
That was full of people!

She has become like a widow
Who was once great among the nations!
She who was a princess among the provinces
Has become a forced laborer

Is it nothing to you, all ye that pass by?
Behold, and see if there by any sorrow
like unto my sorrow...

70 Years in Babylon

The people of Judah were to spend the next 70 years in captivity in Babylon!

Year after year the farmland in Israel was producing an abundant harvest, and the Jews of those days were not anxious to be reminded of, what to them may have been an obscure law of God, which required that they allow the land to remain idle every seventh year.

I'm sure they must have compromised away the law, perhaps by saying that the land produced just as well in the seventh year as it did in the sixth or fifth years.

And to let the land sit idle for the seventh year would be a waste of money and of additional food supplies.

So, for some 490 years the Jews continued to ignore the law that God had given to Moses on Mount Sinai which said in part,

> ...Six years thou shalt sow thy field, and six years thou shalt prune thy vineyard, and gather in the fruit thereof; But in the seventh year shall be a sabbath of rest unto the land, a sabbath for the Lord; thou shalt neither sow thy field, nor prune thy vineyard....
>
> Leviticus 25:1-7

Then in Leviticus 26 verses 2-4, 14, 21,32-35 the Jews are warned that they will suffer judgment if they disobey this commandment:

> ...If ye will not hearken unto Me...and if ye walk contrary unto Me...I will bring the land into desolation...and I will scatter you among the heathen, and will draw out a sword after you: and your lands shall be desolate and your cities waste.

So for 490 years, most of the Jews chose to ignore this commandment, and the consequences were just around the corner.

As prophesied by Jeremiah, the time for Israel's punishment had come.

Jerusalem would be destroyed in a three-stage attack within a ten year period.

The year was 606 B.C. The New Babylonian Empire was reaching its height of power. Because of this, Pharaoh-Necho of Egypt formed an alliance with the Assyrian remnant. Together, they moved northward through Palestine to contest Babylonian rule.

However, as the Egyptians reached Megiddo, King Josiah of Judah and the Judaean army confronted them. It was their hope that they could retain their freedom against this new Egyptian-Assyrian alliance.

It is interesting to note that this confrontation took place at Megiddo. Megiddo was to go down in history as the world's greatest battleground, and the world's greatest battle—the Battle of Armageddon—would one day be fought there.

But at this time, King Josiah was to meet death.

In 2 Kings 23:29 we read:

> In his days Pharaoh-Necho, king of Egypt went up to the king of Assyria to the river Euphrates. And king Josiah went to meet him and when Pharaoh-Necho saw him he killed him at Megiddo.

With Pharaoh-Necho the victor, he made Eliakim the son of Josiah, king, in place of Josiah. He changed his name to Jehoiakim. Jehoiakim was twenty-five years old when he became king and he followed the directives of Pharaoh by giving him all the silver and gold and taxing the land in order to give the money to Pharaoh. He reigned eleven years in Jerusalem and God's Word sums it up in 2 Kings 23:37 when it says:

> He did evil in the sight of the Lord...

Meanwhile, a man by the name of Nabopolassar was having his successes in destroying the great power of Assyria. He also assisted in destroying Nineveh. It was Nabopolassar's son, Nebuchadnezzar, who next met the Egyptian army in

Nebuchadnezzar watches as a soldier blinds the eyes of Zedekiah after he has just witnessed the death of his sons. Man's inhumanity to man will be even greater magnified against the Jewish people by Antichrist during the 7-year Tribulation Period yet to come!

battle and thoroughly defeated Pharaoh-Necho. While in battle he heard that his father had died, so he returned to Babylon to take up his duty as king.

At this time all of Syria, including Judah, had been under Egyptian control, being governed by Jehoiakim. It took Nebuchadnezzar a total of twenty years to completely destroy Jerusalem. There is no doubt that he could have done it sooner, but the consensus of opinion is that he preferred to extract tribute money from the city as long as possible.

Jerusalem's Destruction

About 602 B.C. Jehoiakim revolted against Nebuchadnezzar's Babylonian rule hoping that Egypt would come to the rescue...but Egypt itself was defeated. By the year 598, four years later, Nebuchadnezzar began to pour thousands of soldiers into Palestine, captured Jerusalem, and took King Jehoiakim prisoner. He then put Zedekiah on the throne of Judah and carried 10,000 Jews into bondage. By 586, eleven years later, Zedekiah, a son of Josiah, rebelled against Nebuchadnezzar. As a result of his rebellion, Nebuchadnezzar made Zedekiah watch as he killed his sons before his very eyes. Then Nebuchadnezzar put out Zedekiah's eyes, blinding him. He was then taken to Babylon where he died, after only eleven years of reign.

In fury, Nebuchadnezzar recaptured Jerusalem, burned it to the ground, and destroyed the temple of Solomon.

Nebuchadnezzar could be, perhaps, considered the first type of Antichrist. Two of his famous captives from Jerusalem were Ezekiel and Daniel. And Daniel was to give the most sweeping revelation recorded by any prophet of the Old Testament, concerning the End Times.

It was Nebuchadnezzar's father who had liberated Babylon, making it an independent nation. He bequeathed this crown to his son. Nebuchadnezzar, and thus began his own dynasty.

The time came for Nebuchadnezzar's great inaugural address.

The address was directed to the great god-in-chief of Babylong...Marduk. Part of his inaugural address went like this:

> At thy command, oh merciful Marduk, may the house that I have built endure forever, may I be satiated with its splendour, attain old age therein, with abundant offspring, and receive therein tribute of the kings of all regions, from all mankind.

Jews Deported To Babylon

The first deportation of the Jews from Jerusalem to Babylon included Daniel and his companions. It is interesting to note that because the people of Israel themselves had turned to idolatry, they were now to be carried off, captive to Babylon which was the center of idolatry...and was considered one of the most wicked cities in the ancient world.

In effect, the people of Jerusalem had become worldly and this worldliness thrust them into a period of suffering.

John F. Walvoord, in his book, DANIEL, THE KEY TO PROPHETIC REVELATION, makes a very significant statement when he says:

> Worldly saints do not capture the world but become instead the world's captives.

In his capture of Jerusalem, Nebuchadnezzar ordered that some of the children of Israel should be brought to his court to be trained in royal service.

This perhaps is one of the first kidnappings in history of important personages.

Perhaps Nebuchadnezzar wanted to keep these young people as hostages. He also wanted to train them very carefully so that they could serve him well in his later administration of Jewish affairs.

In selecting these hostages, he wanted to make sure that they were physically perfect, and that they were good looking. They were also to be superior intellectually. Their training was to try to eliminate their previous Jewish culture and teach them "the learning and the tongue of the Chaldeans."

Their education was to cover a three year period. At that time, they would then be ready to take their place of responsibility.

Their's was to be the privilege of eating the king's food which included meat from animals pronounced unclean by the Law of Moses and drinking strong wines.

When this was brought to Daniel's attention he realized that he faced a great problem.

Should he become a worldly saint and compromise his position? Or should he stand on the fundamentals of the faith and risk his life?

Life was considered very cheap in Babylon, and everyone was subject to the whims of the king.

Daniel's Health Test

But Daniel had an idea. He suggested that the steward allow him to conduct a ten day test.

Daniel and his companions were to eat what grows out of the ground, that is, vegetables.

The other servants were to eat the king's regular selection of food.

At the conclusion of the test, Daniel and his companions not only looked better but also were fuller in flesh than those who had continued to eat the king's food.

Perhaps this would be a good object lesson even for Christians today in light of highly processed foods and the multiplicity of sweet desserts which tempt many.

At about twenty years of age Daniel and his companions completed their three years of education for Nebuchadnezzar's court. In fact, Nebuchadnezzar was highly pleased with them because he found them ten times better than all the magicians and astrologers that were in his realm. The time would soon come for Daniel to be tested.

In the second year of the reign of Nebuchadnezzar, he began to have dreams and had difficulty sleeping.

Whether he had late midnight snacks or not is not told, but we do know that these dreams disturbed him greatly. One commentator remarked that Nebuchadnezzar did a thing which no believer in God should ever dream of doing... that is Nebuchadnezzar took his problems to bed with him.

Disturbing Dreams

In order to get an interpretation of his dream, Nebuchadnezzar gathered together all the wise men on his staff. They were divided into four different classifications: (1) the magicians, (2) the astrologers, (3) the sorcerers, and (4) the Chaldeans.

The Chaldeans were wise men who came originally from southern Babylon.

The Chaldeans acted as spokesmen for the entire group and as was typical in those days, addressed the king with an elaborate, oriental courtesy, "Oh king, live forever."

Nebuchadnezzar not only wanted them to interpret his dream but he also wanted them to tell him *what* he had dreamed.

Of course, the wise men could not tell him what he had dreamed. This angered Nebuchadnezzar who threatened to cut the wise men into pieces. This was not an uncommon cruelty.

Nebuchadnezzar, in a fitful sleep, dreams of a large statue so brilliant that it caused him to cringe. The statue was to depict the down trodding of Israel by the Gentiles.

Those who came under Nebuchadnezzar's displeasure were often executed by being dismembered, and their houses were ruined.

The wise men had a choice—either tell Nebuchadnezzar what he dreamed and receive gifts and rewards and great honor—or fail, which would mean a horrible death.

Nebuchadnezzar believed that if they had a genuine supernatural ability to interpret a dream, they should also have this same ability to reveal its content.

The wise men, of course, could not tell the content of Nebuchadnezzar's dream. Not only could they not tell the content, but they stated:

> There is not a man on earth who could
> declare the matter for the king...
>
> Daniel 2:10

At this statement Nebuchadnezzar signed a decree "to destroy all the wise men of Babylon." This not only meant the wise men who had an audience with Nebuchadnezzar, but also Daniel and his companions. No doubt this was quite a shock to Daniel and his companions to come, within a three year period, from a select group of servants chosen by Nebuchadnezzar, and now to feel the wrath of this same man and be placed under the edict of death by dismemberment.

Daniel Interprets Dream

This caused Daniel and his companions to pray for wisdom. And Daniel had a vision one night in answer to his prayers.

Daniel was able to tell Nebuchadnezzar not only what he dreamed, but also the interpretation of the dream.

Briefly, what Nebuchadnezzar saw was the majestic procession of four great world empires. He saw their destruction. He then saw their replacement by a fifth empire, a kingdom from heaven.

In Nebuchadnezzar's dream there was a large statue which had an appearance so brilliant that Nebuchadnezzar cringed before this unusual spectacle. The head of the statue was fine gold, the chest and arms were silver, the belly and thighs were brass, the legs were of iron, and the feet were part iron and part clay.

Daniel goes on to explain that the head of gold is a refer-

The Image of Daniel 2

606 ± B.C.
Gold—Nebuchadnezzar's
Babylon (Unquestioned
obedience to one absolute
sovereign)

536 ± B.C.
Silver—The dual Empire of
the Medes & Persians
(The 2 arms!)

336 B.C.
Copper—The Greek
Empire

200 ± B.C.
Iron Legs United—
Roman Republic & Empire

300 ± A.D.
Iron Legs Divided—
Western & Eastern
Roman Empire

476 & 1453 A.D. (They fall)

Iron Legs Cracking—
European States

Iron & Clay Feet—End-time
Lawlessness (Communism)?

10 Toes—Revived Rome
Confederacy

A.D.?

ence to the empire controlled by Nebuchadnezzar—the empire of Babylon. This is the first kingdom described.

The second and third kingdoms were to be inferior to Babylon in their rule over the entire earth.

The second kingdom was to be the kingdom of Medo-Persia.

The third kingdom would be Greece.

So we start out with a kingdom represented by gold, and proceed to a kingdom represented by silver, and then a third kingdom represented by brass. These show the deterioration of metals from gold, which is considered the most precious, down to the less precious silver and brass. This was a symbolism of kingdoms which would be inferior to the kingdom of Babylon—but yet, quite strong and quite dominant in their power over the entire earth.

Subsequent history confirmed that both the Medo-Persian empire, and the empire of Alexander of Greece which followed, lacked the central authority which characterized the Babylonian Empire.

Of all the empires, the fourth kingdom in Nebuchadnezzar's dream, which is represented by the iron legs and the feet of the statue made of iron and clay, is the most important.

The strength of the legs, being iron, well represents Ancient Rome since the Roman legions were noted for their ability to crush all resistance with an iron heel.

However, as we near the End Times we find that the iron attempts to mix with the clay, and this mixture in the ten toes, or ten latter day nations becomes a very weak mixture which has a tendency to crumble and fall apart.

We are witnessing such incompatible mixtures today, as with the mixture of democracy with dictatorship. A new 20th century word—co-existence—is one that made it possible for the United States democracy to recognize Red China, a dictatorship.

This same strange iron and clay relationship exists with Russia and the United States.

What Daniel seems to be telling us is that the final fourth world empire at the end of this present age will be a unity that is yet divided. We will see forces from throughout the bounds of the ancient Roman Empire (the Iron) join with Antichrist—who will be ruler of the Mediterranean in a total supremacy.

Forces from the south, east, and north will contend with him. This will culminate in the great Battle of Armageddon. It will be at this time that Daniel's ten toes—which are kingdoms existing side by side—will be destroyed by one sudden, catastrophic blow. Nothing like this has yet occurred. This is prophecy yet to be fulfilled during the Tribulation Period.

During Christ's life on earth, the Roman Empire had spread over in the east and the west, and included Syria, Egypt, as well as Africa, and the European nations.

In the End Times as well, this same dominance of territory will exist.

Nebuchadnezzar was so overwhelmed by the significance of the image he had dreamed and Daniel's interpretation, that he fell on his face and started to worship Daniel. It was not that he was worshipping Daniel, but rather Daniel's God. A similar instance would occur later, when Alexander the Great bowed before the high priest of the Jews. When one of his generals asked him why he would bow to a Jew, Alexander replied:

> It was not before him that I prostrated myself, but the God of whom he has the honour to be the high priest.

Daniel started out as an obscure Jewish captive, and if he had compromised with his beliefs, he probably would have remained an obscure Jewish captive, and would have been lost to history like so many others.

But when Daniel stood up for what he believed in, even though such assertions might mean death, the Bible reveals that he played an important part in the revelation of prophetic history.

A Golden Image Erected

Apparently, Nebuchadnezzar had a short memory, for after a period of about twenty years he decided to erect a golden image on the plain of Dura. Most scholars believe that Dura was an area located six miles southeast of Babylon. It occupied a mound which consisted of a large square of brick construction which would have ideally served as a base for such an image as Nebuchadnezzar erected.

According to Daniel chapter 3, this image of gold was extremely high—60 cubits (90 feet) high, in fact, and 6 cubits (9 feet) broad at the base. It must have been a very impressive sight as one suddenly came upon this on the expansive plain of Dura.

When one examines the number of cubits—as cubits were the unit of measure in those days—we come across a very surprising revelation. These numbers together, 60 by 6 by 6 suggest the number 666, the number of man as written in Revelation 13:18.

How prophetic this number would be and will be in the End Times during the Tribulation Period, and yet this particular incident occured in 585 B.C. —over 2500 years ago.

Since Daniel had told Nebuchadnezzar that his kingdom was the strongest and was symbolized by gold, it might have been Nebuchadnezzar's idea to erect this very unusual statue to commemorate this event a few years later.

This was going to be an occasion to remember, and Nebuchadnezzar ordered all of the important people of the government to be there at the official dedication of this image. This was to include the princes, the governors, the captains, the judges, the treasurers, the counsellors, and the sheriffs.

I'm sure that such a display of officials reflected the power of Nebuchadnezzar's empire. This was to be a dramatic occasion. The Babylonian symphonic orchestra was there with its cornets, its flutes, harp, dulcimer, and other musical instruments.

The Test

At the sound of this musical salute, everyone was to fall down and worship the golden image. It was made plain that anyone who would not obey this command to fall down and worship the image would be cast immediately into a burning, fiery furnace.

Nebuchadnezzar had many means of sadistic tortures, and added to his execution by dismemberment was also the alternative of being thrown into a fiery furnace. In Persia, there were many ovens of similar nature used for the execution of criminals. The furnace was so designed that the king could see what was happening inside the furnace.

If you were present in this great crowd at that time, what would have been your decision? Would you fall down and worship the image, or remain standing, knowing that you would be thrown into a fiery furnace?

Here again, there was no room for compromise, and Daniel's three companions were the only ones who did not bow down—Shadrach, Meshach, and Abed-nego.

Nebuchadnezzar was very angry, but decided to give them a second chance because they were from the original select group of Jews that Nebuchadnezzar admired. Again, the three companions of Daniel had the opportunity to change their mind and worship the image. Again they refused.

This time, Nebuchadnezzar was full of fury, or in today's language, "fit to be tied."

So angry was he, that he ordered the soldiers to heat the furnace seven times hotter.

If he realized what he was saying, he would have suggested a slow fire, as this would have been far more torture for the three, rather than an extremely hot fire. Imagine Nebuchadnezzar standing near the furnace with the three companions of Daniel, surrounded by guards, as the soldiers stoked the furnace until it got extremely hot. This must have been a moment of great tension, and a moment of great faith and trust on the part of those three.

The Fiery Furnace

The time came for their execution. They were bound with their coats and hats on as well as their other garments, and *thrown* into the midst of the furnace.

The amazing thing is that the fire was so hot that the men who cast the three men into the furnace were actually killed by the flames. The three should have suffered an almost instant death. At least that's what Nebuchadnezzar thought. And he felt his eyes were deceiving him when he asked the question:

> Did not we cast three men bound into the midst of the fire?

He was told that, yes, three men were cast bound, into the fire.

And Nebuchadnezzar answered:

I see four men loose.

Instead of writhing in anguish in the flames, the three men were actually walking about in the fire and making no attempt to come out.

When Nebuchadnezzar asked them to come out, everyone noticed that not a hair on their head had been singed, nor was the smell of fire upon them.

Nebuchadnezzar had once again seen the power of God working...but he was soon to forget.

In Nebuchadnezzar's early reign over Babylon he was very active in conquering vast territories. Now that these territories had been made secure—Nebuchadnezzar decided to fulfill other avenues of desire. It was his desire to make Babylon one of the most fabulous cities of the ancient world.

Daniel Interprets New Dream

But again, in Daniel chapter 4, Nebuchadnezzar had a dream. He saw a tree standing by itself, and dominating the view because of its great height. This green giant grew so high until it was visible all over the entire earth. Suddenly the tree is cut down. Its branches are cut off, and its leaves are shaken off, and its fruit is scattered. The stump of the tree is bound with a band of iron and brass. Again Daniel is called in, and again Daniel interprets this dream.

Daniel tells Nebuchadnezzar that the tree represents Nebuchadnezzar. He also told him that one day he would be cut down and driven from ordinary association with men and that he would dwell with the beasts of the field. He is also told, however, that the kingdom will be restored to him at a later date.

So proud was he of his accomplishments in building Babylon that the Bible tells us in Daniel 4:30:

...Is this not Babylon the great, which
I myself have built as a royal residence
by the might of my power and for the
glory of my majesty?

Babylon as it probably looked in the days of Nebuchadnezzar and as it looks today!

All that is left of the once great palaces of Babylon!

His father Nabopolassar, had laid plans for the recon-
struction of Babylon, but it was Nebuchadnezzar who
used his long reign of 43 years to carry these plans to completion. This magnificent new Babylon was surrounded by
a wall 56 miles in circumference, so broad that a 4-horse
chariot could be driven along the top, and enclosing an
area of some 200 square miles. Through the center of the
town ran the palm-fringed Euphrates, busy with commerce.
Most of the buildings were brick, but the bricks were
often faced with enamel tiles of brilliant blue, yellow, or
white. Nearly all the bricks that have been recovered from
the site of Babylon, bear the proud inscription:

I am Nebuchadnezzar, king of Babylon.

The first sight a visitor would see upon entering Babylon
was an immense and lofty ziggurat—a tower—rising in
seven stages of gleaming enamel to a height of 650 feet,
crowned with a shrine containing a massive table of solid
gold, and an ornate bed on which, each night, some woman
slept to await the pleasure of the god.

This structure, taller than the pyramids of Egypt, was
surely a "tower of Babel."

South of this ziggurat stood the gigantic Temple of Marduk,
deity of Babylon. Connecting the temples was a spacious,
"Sacred Way." At one end of the "Sacred Way" rose the
magnificent Ishtar Gate, a massive double portal of re-
splendent tiles adorned with enameled flowers.

Nebuchadnezzar BUILDS one of
Seven Wonders of the World

North of the Tower of Babel was a mound called Kasar, on
which Nebuchadnezzar built the most imposing of his
palaces. Nearby, supported on a succession of superim-
posed circular colonnades, were the famous hanging gardens. The Greeks included this among the Seven Wonders
of the World.

Will Durant, in his book, OUR ORIENTAL HERITAGE,
gives a comprehensive description of Babylon. Nebuchadnezzar had built the hanging gardens for one of his
wives, who, unaccustomed to the hot sun and dust of Babylon, pined for the verdant green of her native hills. The
topmost terrace was covered with rich soil to the depth
of many feet.

Hydraulic engines concealed in the columns and manned by shifts of slaves carried water from the Euphrates to the higher tiers of the garden. Imagine here, 75 feet above the ground, in the cool shade of tall trees, and surrounded by exotic shrubs and fragrant flowers, the ladies of the royal harem walking unveiled enjoying one of the Seven Wonders of the World.

The shrine of Marduk was approximately 300 feet high, and could be seen 60 miles away in every direction.

The Fall of A King

When Nebuchadnezzar made the boast:

> Is not this great Babylon, that I
> have built for the house of My
> kingdom, by the might of my power,
> and for the honour of my majesty

...his transition from sanity to insanity was immediate.

Suddenly he was reduced from a man of great power and majesty to the level of an ordinary beast. In today's current world we have witnessed equally as sudden losses of power.

The details of Nebuchadnezzar's period of trial are not told to us in the Scripture.

Perhaps Nebuchadnezzar was kept in the palace and looked after by Daniel.

Minutes before, he was a ruling monarch. Suddenly he was eating grass like an ox.

After seven years, God laid His hands on Nebuchadnezzar, and brought back his sanity. This is the last we read in the Scriptures of Nebuchadnezzar. He lived about one year after his return to the throne in Babylon. During his reign, he was successful in completely demolishing Jerusalem, tearing down its walls, and destroying the Temple. Leading citizens were deported to Babylon, and a broken remnant was left in Judah.

Because of his lust for power, three dreams brought him face to face with God. Nebuchadnezzar died in 562 B.C. Whether Nebuchadnezzar accepted God as his Lord and Savior, or whether he simply accepted Him as one more powerful than he...only eternity will tell.

ENTER THE MEDES AND THE PERSIANS

The Babylonians, under Nebuchadnezzar, were the first of 6 empires to totally dominate Jerusalem and Israel...in Daniel's *times of the Gentiles.* They accomplished this through conquering and subduing all of Judah and the regions surrounding it.

The second group were the Medes and the Persians.

Babylon (the head of gold in the image of Daniel 2), had kings whose power was absolute.

> *...whomever he wished he feared and trembled*
> *before him; whomever he wished he killed,*
> *and whomever he wished he spared alive;*
> *and whomever he wished he elevated,*
> *and whomever he wished he humbled.*
> *(Daniel 5:19)*

But in Medo-Persia the *law* was superior to the king. The king could not alter a law...even if he thought the change to be better for his subjects! Read Daniel 6:1-16. Although Darius wished to spare Daniel from the lions' den, he was powerless to alter the law.

In fact the commissioners, jealous of Daniel's power, tricked Darius into putting into law a command that every subject should worship solely Darius.

The Law Of The Medes And The Persians

Even though Darius realized he had been fooled...he was forced to follow his own law when the commissioners reminded him:

> Did you not sign an injunction that any man who makes a petition to any god or man besides you, O king, for thirty days, is to be cast into the lions' den?

> The king answered and said, "The statement is true, according to the law of the Medes and Persians, which may not be revoked."
>
> (Daniel 6:12)

We will see that as each of these kingdoms subsequently ruled over Israel, each kingdom was weaker than the preceding one. So while in Babylon the king was absolute ruler ...in the case of the second power, the Medes and the Persians, the king was powerless to break the law!

In today's twentieth century with the past scandal of Watergate, perhaps many would wish again for the rigid law of the Medes and Persians. They desire a code of law so firm that no leader would dare to trespass it!

The Medes and Persians are represented in the image of Daniel 2 as the dual empire of silver and is the breast with its two arms in this image.

Let's examine their background.

Who were the Medes? The Medes came from an area we now call Iran. Our first known reference of them occurs in 836 B.C. as paying tribute to the Assyrian conqueror Shalmaneser II. Because of the abundance of minerals, animals and birds...the inhabitants of the land of Media (the Medes), enjoyed comparative luxurious living.

It is interesting to note that they became famous for their horses. At one time they paid a yearly tribute to Assyria of 3000 horses, plus 4000 mules and almost 100,000 sheep.

The Medes were powerful warriors, extremely skillful in the use of the bow. And, in fact, although Media was at one time simply a province of Assyria, the growing Medes eventually overthrew Babylon. In those days such an invasion was thought fantastic and impossible...like a David fighting a Goliath. Imagine for a moment, as an example Rhode Island (one state) overthrowing the rest of the United States!

Listen to the prophecy of Isaiah 13:17-19:

> Behold, I am going to stir up the Medes against them,
> Who will not value silver or take pleasure in gold,
> And their bows will mow down the young men,
> They [the Medes] will not even have compassion
>   on the fruit of the womb,
> Nor will their eye pity children.
>
> And Babylon, the beauty of kingdoms, the glory of
>   the Chaldeans' pride,
> Will be as when God overthrew Sodom and Gomorrah.

And it was this nation, which eventually merged with Persia, that was to control Israel for almost 50 years!

As previously stated, the Medes were a people of affluence. To Persia, the Medes gave their Aryan language, their alphabet of 36 characters. They replaced clay with parchment and used the pen as writing materials.

A Rapid Rise...A Rapid Fall

Although their rise was rapid...the degeneration of the Medes was more rapid.

Astyages, King of the Medes (ca. 560 B.C.), surrounded by wealth that had come too suddenly, let the morals of the nation slip. The upper class became the slaves of fashion and luxury. The women covered themselves with cosmetics and jewelry. The men wore embroidered trousers. Even the horses were often richly adorned in gold. These people who in previous years were content to ride in crude wagons now rode in expensive chariots from feast to feast.

While earlier kings had prided themselves on justice, King Astyages, angry at Harpagus, a Median General, forced on Harpagus a cruel punishment.

Astyages killed the son of Harpagus...then had him dismembered...and served the headless and cut-up boy on a platter and forced Harpagus to eat some of the flesh. General Harpagus ate, saying that whatever a king did was agreeable to him. Later, however, a vengeful General Harpagus aided Cyrus to depose Astyages.

Cyrus gives Zerubbabel, governor of the Jewish colony,
the golden vessels which Nebuchadnezzar had taken from
the temple in Jerusalem.

The Medes had established a strong empire east of the Tigris, which included the Persians. It was the Medes who aided the Chaldeans (Babylonians) in the destruction of Nineveh in 612 B.C.

The Success Of Cyrus

Sixty years after the fall of Nineveh, the energetic leader of the little kingdom of Anshan, Cyrus by name, united the Persian tribes into a nation and threw off the rule of the Medes, to whom they had been subject.

The rapid success of Cyrus so alarmed the peoples to the west that Lydia (today's Western Turkey), Chaldea (Babylon) and Egypt combined against him. Cyrus promptly marched his army all the way to Lydia, captured the capital, Sardis. Within five years the little Persian kingdom had conquered Asia Minor to the Mediterranean Sea and had become the strongest power in the Near East.

Fulfilling the prophecy of Daniel 5:28, King Belshazzar (grandson of Nebuchadnezzar), was slain and the army of Cyrus entered Babylon.

In contrast to the cruelty of the Assyrians, the Persian kings treated conquered rulers and populations humanely, spared cities from destruction, and left the inhabitants in peace. Cyrus believed that various peoples of his empire should be left free in their religious worship and beliefs.

For two hundred years the Jews had awaited the fulfilment of God's prophecy that they could once again return to Jerusalem.

A Free Trip Home

Now, with Cyrus, king of Persia...the time had come. Cyrus issued a proclamation permitting captive Jews to return to Jerusalem.

Cyrus' first call was made in 537 B.C. But no more than 50,000 Jews responded to this opportunity! Cyrus gave Zerubbabel, governor of the Jewish colony, the golden vessels which Nebuchadnezzar had taken from the temple in Jerusalem (Zechariah 4:9). The trip from Babylon to Jerusalem was through 700 miles of trackless desert!

You will recall that at the time of the captivity, just 70 years before only the better class of people were taken into Babylon. The majority of Jews were left in Jerusalem to suffer the trials inflicted by Nebuchadnezzar's army.

Now, some 70 years later, those in Babylon had established themselves, built homes, and for the most part, were content to stay in Babylon. They were not anxious to take a 700 mile trip and face the uncertainties of Jerusalem.

Could this not be compared to today's dilemma? Since 1948 the people of Israel have fought bitterly for every square inch of land. The brunt of the birth of this nation has been borne by the refugees from Europe and now by the sabra... Israelis who were born in Palestine. Most who serve in the kibbutz communities in Israel are those who suffered under Hitler's Germany. Very few American Jews, although they have longed for a time when Israel would be back in her land, have themselves migrated to their home land.

In the United States, they have built homes and prosperous businesses. And to travel 7000 or 8000 miles to a land where they would have to work with their hands, and live frugally does not appear too enticing.

Not only did Cyrus provide money for rebuilding the temple in Jerusalem, but he also provided traveling expenses.

Would You Accept The Offer?

Suppose next Sunday in your church the Pastor would make this announcement:

> The President of the United States has issued the following decree: All Christians who wish to reside in the Holy Land will now be allowed to. The United States will provide all the funds to build local churches in Israel, and provide for your Pastor to transfer to that church. Every member will also be given free transportation to Israel.

Would you take up the President on that offer?

That's exactly the situation the Jews found themselves. Not quite exactly. We are aware of what Israel is like. We can fly there in a matter of hours! The Jews in Babylon did not know what they would find in Jerusalem. And it would take 700 miles of travel over a barren desert (3 or 4 months time) to reach their goal.

Some 60 years after the first contingent of Jews had reached Jerusalem...these colonists were still struggling.

This time King Artaxerxes was King of Persia. And Ezra

had returned to Babylon to get more volunteers. This time *only 1700* Jews made the journey to Jerusalem.

Sin In The Camp

When Ezra returned to Jerusalem he discovered that the Jews had intermarried. While all classes of people were involved in this sin, the political leaders (princes) were guilty of having set this standard.

Ezra was so upset he tore his clothing, and pulled some of his hair from his head. In those days tearing of garments was a sign of deep affliction, and plucking of hair and beard was a sign of moral indignation.

Finally at evening he stood and prayed to the Lord:

...O my God, I am ashamed and embarrassed
    to lift up my face to Thee,
    for our iniquities have risen above our heads...

Since the days of our fathers to this day we have
    been in great guilt,
    and on account of our iniquities we, our kings
    and our priests have been given into the hand
    of the kings of the lands, to the sword,
    to captivity, and to plunder and to open shame,
    as it is this day.

But now for a brief moment grace has been shown
    from the Lord our God, to leave us an escaped rem-
    nant and to give us a peg [Jerusalem] in His holy
    place...

For we are slaves; yet in our bondage, our God has not
    forsaken us, but has extended lovingkindness to us
    in the sight of the kings of Persia, to give us reviving
    to raise up the house of our God, to restore its ruins,
    and to give us a wall in Judah and Jerusalem.

And now, our God, what shall we say after this? For
    we have forsaken Thy commandments...

                  (Ezra 9:6-10)

The Jews had been in bondage for centuries of sufferings under the Assyrians and Babylonians...and now after this brief moment of relative freedom under the Medes and Persians...some 80 years (as described in verse 8 above) they were in danger of forfeiting it all.

Ezra, at the water gate, rebukes the Israelites for disobeying God and urges them to repent.

The Confession At Water Gate

While Ezra was praying, men, women and children gathered around him and began to weep. One member confessed his sin (Ezra 10:2).

Ezra began a fast. Meanwhile a proclamation was issued that all the exiles in Judah and Jerusalem should assemble in Jerusalem within three days. Those who refused would forfeit all their possessions and be exiled.

On December 8, 457 B.C. a vast multitude of Jews gathered in the open space in front of the Water Gate to hear Ezra's message...a message that those who sinned by marrying those from foreign lands should repent and separate themselves from this unholy alliance. Such marriages were absolutely forbidden to Israel under the Old Testament Law.

As they sat in the open square at the Water Gate a severe storm came. The rain poured in torrents and the entire group shivered in the rain as they were literally soaked to the skin—drenched!

Ezra's command to: "...make confession to the Lord God of your fathers, and do His will" (Ezra 10:11)...was followed. Everyone who had a heathen wife met before a panel of judges and separation of the intermarriages was completed after four months of examinations.

In 1972 another Watergate made the headlines and the multiple sins of the leaders of our nation were agonized in newspaper headlines for many years after. Why? Because the nation lacked an Ezra to point out sin as sin...without compromise...and the people lacked the desire to stand before God and repent!

When Nehemiah came to Jerusalem in 445 B.C., Ezra had been there for 13 years. Ezra was a priest. Nehemiah was a civil governor. Nehemiah had come under the authority of the king of Persia to build the walls of Jerusalem. He accomplished this in 52 days because

The people had a mind to work. (Nehemiah 4:6)

Under Babylonian rule, Israel was not only dominated but also persecuted. Under the rule of the Medes and the Persians, Israel was conquered but allowed to practice her faith. Now would come further bondage under the heavy hand of Greece!

6

THE POWER OF ALEXANDER THE GREAT

The Grecian Empire, under Alexander the Great, was the third power to dominate Israel in Daniel's *times of the Gentiles.*

Of the first three kingdoms, Alexander the Great controlled the greatest territory. Alexander started in Greece and Macedon (Northern Greece) but he conquered all the territories of the Babylonians and the Medes and Persians and even part of India. Macedon, known also as Macedonia, is now a region which includes parts of Greece, Bulgaria and Yugoslavia.

It is interesting to note that between chapters 6 and 7 of Ezra, three great world battles were fought:

1. The Battle at Marathon   490 B.C.
   The Greeks defeated the Persians

2. The Battle of Salamis   480 B.C.
   The Greeks defeated the Persians in a naval battle.

3. The Battle of Thermopylae   480 B.C.
   The Persians defeated the Spartans
         (The Spartans were from South Greece)

Also during this 58-year time period (516-458 B.C.) both Confucius and Buddha died (and they did not rise again!). This is the time period in which the book of Esther takes place.

While the Medes and the Persians represented the breast and two arms of silver in the image of Daniel 2...the Greek Empire represented the abdomen of copper in the image of Daniel 2.

Alexander the Great is pictured in Daniel 8:5 prophetically as the he goat:

> While I was observing, behold, a male goat was coming from the west over the surface of the whole earth without touching the ground; and the goat had a conspicuous horn between his eyes.

Daniel continued to describe here what would happen down through the middle of the 2nd Century B.C.—*over 400 years prior to when the actual event took place!*

> And he [Alexander the Great] came up to the ram that had two horns...[the kings of Media and Persia] [the Medes and the Persians].

> And I saw him come beside the ram...
> and he struck the ram and shattered his two horns, and the ram had no strength to withstand him... and there was none to rescue the ram from his power.
>
> (Daniel 8:6-7)

In four major wars Alexander the Great crushed the power of the Medes and Persians:

1. River Granicus Campaign   334 B.C.
   Alexander the Great led his forces into Asia Minor (Turkey) and defeated the Persian forces. Figuratively speaking he moved with such rapidity "... without touching the ground" (Daniel 8:5).

2. Issus Campaign   333 B.C.
   In this ancient town (now a part of Turkey), Alexander the Great defeated Darius, III of Persia.

3. The Campaign against Egypt   332 B.C.
   Moving with swiftness, Alexander the Great quickly subdued Egypt.

4. The Campaign at Arbela (Gaugamela)   331 B.C.
   In the most spectacular battle Alexander the Great fought, he finally crushed the empire of the Medes and Persians!

Let's see how the people of Israel were affected as they suddenly found themselves no longer under the bondage of the Medes and Persians, but under the dominion of the Greeks.

Men of Alexander's armies. Armor was made of leather reinforced to deflect arrows and to dull the jabs of enemy swords. The breastplate was made of overlapping metal scales.

In the middle of the fourth century B.C., the Persian empire was the greatest empire the world had yet seen. It stretched from Asia Minor to India and from Egypt to what is now known as Russia. It was just 150 years since Persia's army had burned Athens. The tide, however, was to turn, and soon the Jews were to have new rulers...the Greeks.

The Path Of Blazing Glory

Philip II, intent on uniting Greece, lost his life through an assassin's knife. His son, Alexander the Great, some 2300 years ago, was to blaze across three continents, smashing the Persian empire.

Alexander the Great had a wild energy. When a march became boring he would shoot arrows at passing objects. If he lived today he probably would have entered the Indianapolis 500 auto races. One of his favorite pastimes was alighting from and remounting his chariot at full speed!

He liked hard work and dangerous wars. He laughed at some of his generals who had so many servants that they themselves could find nothing to do (Is this a picture of some of your own congressmen?).

He hated to waste time sleeping. And he admonished his lazy generals saying: "I wonder that you with your experience do not know that those who work sleep more soundly than those for whom other people work. Have you yet to learn that the greatest need after our victories is to avoid the vices and the weaknesses of those whom we have conquered?"

Alexander the Great despised rich foods and partially because of this enjoyed good health...a wise tip for all of us.

You may not realize that it was Alexander the Great who introduced into Europe the custom of shaving the beard. He believed that whiskers offered too ready a handle for an enemy to grasp. And this custom found its way not only throughout Europe but eventually even into America.

Plutarch said Alexander the Great had a violent thirst for learning. He loved to read.

"For my part," he wrote to Aristotle, "I had rather surpass others in the knowledge of what is excellent, than in the extent of my power and dominion."

Alexander the Great, however, despite the above statement, so loved war with its frenzy and excitement and glory that his mind never knew an hour of peace.

To Conquer The World

When Alexander the Great became ruler of Greece he found himself at the head of a tottering empire. He found his state treasury some $3 million in the red! He promptly borrowed some $5 million and set out to conquer the world ...beginning first with Persia.

Persia had some million fighting men available. Alexander's basic force was only about 40,000 infantry and 5000 cavalry. Many of his own countrymen were not fond of him. In fact it was said that half of Greece was praying that Alexander would soon be killed. This was no doubt partially because Alexander earlier had subdued rebellious Thebes (in Greece, not the Thebes of Egypt). He slew all the men and sold all of the rebellious town's Greek women and children into slavery. No wonder many Greeks, as well as Persians, feared and hated him.

In 334 B.C. Alexander started out on his conquests. It would be an eleven year expedition that would end in his death. He would never see his home again.

Alexander the Great of Greece versus Darius of Persia! How could such a small army defeat the empire of Darius III?

It's an age old story. Persia, resting on her laurels as world conqueror for almost a century, descended into corruption and apathy.

Eating became the principal occupation of the aristocracy. Previously they were content to eat one brief meal a day. Now they still ate one meal...but it lasted from noon to night!

They stocked their kitchens with a thousand delicacies. Oftentimes they served an entire animal to their guest. They stuffed themselves with rich rare meats. Drunkenness became a common vice of every class.

PERSIA'S CORRUPTION

This corruption began with Xerxes I, king of Persia...known as Ahasuerus in the Book of Esther.

Queen Vashti refuses her King's command.

Xerxes was a handsome, tall man whose time was divided by many mistresses.

In the third year of his reign he was planning for a campaign against Greece...the sea battle of Salamis (480 B.C.). Xerxes (Ahasuerus) had spent four years in preparation for this war.

In preparation for this expedition Xerxes planned a special banquet in which all the nobels and princes would attend. The banquet was to be held at the royal palace at Shushan ...the winter residence of Persian kings. This was no ordinary banquet. It was to last 180 days!

This was the age of gluttony and in between wars...men spent their time on food and women. The men feasted in the palace gardens.

But Queen Vashti recognized that modesty is the crown jewel of womanhood. And she entertained the women privately in the quietness of her apartments.

On the seventh day of a subsequent special feast, when Xerxes was drunk, he ordered Queen Vashti to come to him and display her beauty to the palace servants and cabinet officials.

And the king loved Esther more than all the women, and she found favor and kindness with him more than all the virgins, so that he set the royal crown on her head and made her queen...(Esther 2:17).

This was an unusual demand for a Persian king to request that his Queen expose herself at a banquet of drunken revellers. The king, in his sober mood, would have never tolerated such a request.

Queen Vashti refused!

The king, in his drunken stupor, was furious. Queens were subject to the same complete will of the monarch as were slaves.

Xerxes consulted with his lawyers, who replied:

> If it please the king, let there go a royal commandment
> from him, and let it be written among the laws
> of the Persians and the Medes that it may not be
> altered,
> That Vashti come no more before King Ahasuerus;
> and let the king give her royal estate unto another
> who is better than she.
>
> (Esther 1:19)

Their reasoning:

> For the queen's conduct will become known to all the
> women causing them to look with contempt on
> their husbands...when the king's edict is heard
> throughout all his kingdom...then all women will
> give honor to their husbands, great and small.
>
> (Esther 1:17,20)

To find a replacement the King had a beauty contest. At
the palace was a Jew named Mordecai. He had been captured when Jerusalem was destroyed by Nebuchadnezzar
and had been exiled to Babylon. He had not, for some
reason, taken the opportunity to return to Jerusalem.

He had a young cousin, an orphan girl, whose name was
Hadassah (Esther). Esther joined the other young ladies
at the palace in a run-off contest. Each girl received 6
months of beauty treatments with oil of myrrh. This was
followed by 6 months with special perfumes and ointments.

Then each girl spent one night with King Ahasuerus
(Esther 2:14).

Esther As Queen

The king finally decided to select Esther as his queen...
little realizing that she was a Jewess.

Meanwhile, Xerxes (Ahasuerus) has made his historic
attack on Greece with some 5 million men...suffering an
awesome defeat! Two years after this defeat he married
Esther. She was to be queen for 13 years...and it was no
doubt because of her lasting pro-Jewish influence that
Nehemiah 35 years later under the next Persian king was
able to rebuild Jerusalem (Nehemiah 2:1-8).

Esther confronts Haman in front of Xerxes (King Ahasuerus).

(Esther 7:3-4)

It wasn't long before the chief villain appears...Haman. Xerxes made Haman what would be the equivalent of prime minister. Haman, an Amalekite, was a natural enemy of Israel. Haman's hatred of the Jews was further increased by the fact that Mordecai refused to bow before him and show him the respect of Prime Minister.

Haman plotted to have a wholesale massacre of the Jews because of Mordecai's refusal to give divine honor to a man.

Haman decided to throw dice to select a day of massacre. The day selected was March 13, just 10 months away. Haman tried to prove all Jews were disloyal subjects. He even offered to pay Xerxes almost $20 million as a bribe.

The King signed a decree ordering all men, women, and children who were Jews to be killed...their property taken.

How similar this is to World War 2 days during the reign of Hitler in Germany!

The Strategy Of Esther

When Mordecai revealed the edict to Queen Esther, Esther knew what had to be done—she must see the King.

But she could not enter unsummoned to the King's presence. In Persia the King's power was absolute. He could kill with a word, without trial or reason. In those days, punishments meted out included branding, maiming, mutilation, blinding, imprisonment or death. Death was carried out by poisoning, impaling, stoning or crucifixion usually with the head down. In some cases, death was meted out by burying the body up to the head, then crushing the head between huge stones and smothering the victim in hot ashes.

Esther realized what happened to the previous queen, Queen Vashti. Who could tell what this fickle monarch would now do to her?

The First Banquet

Knowing Xerxes loved banquets, she invited him to a banquet. She also invited Haman. Keeping Xerxes in an expectant mood...she did not reveal her request that night... but invited the King along with Haman to still another banquet on the following evening.

Mordecai rides in triumph in place of Haman.

(Esther 6:8-10)

Haman was so pleased he told his wife:

> Even Esther the queen let no one but me come
> with the king to the banquet which she had pre-
> pared; and tomorrow also I am invited by her with
> the king.
>
> (Esther 5:12)

To which his wife, Zeresh, encouraged:

> Have a gallows 75-foot-high made and in the
> morning ask the king to have Mordecai hanged
> on it.
>
> (Esther 5:14)

The gallows was made.

The night before the banquet, Xerxes had a sleepless
night. So he had the book of records read to him and realized that Mordecai had some years before thwarted a plot
to kill Xerxes. He therefore called Haman to ask his advice
on what honor should be given a man for great devotion to
duty.

Haman, believing Xerxes was referring to his own zealousness, suggested that such a man should wear a

> royal robe which the king has worn,
> and the horse on which the king has ridden,
> and on whose head a royal crown has been placed;
>
> and let the robe and the horse be handed over
> to one of the king's most nobel princes and
> let them array the man whom the king desires
> to honor and lead him on horseback through
> the city square, and proclaim before him,
> Thus it shall be done to the man whom the
> king desires to honor.
>
> (Esther 6:8-9)

Then to the astonishment of Haman, Haman is directed to:

> Take quickly the robes and the horse, as you have
> said, and do so for Mordecai, the Jew, who is sitting
> at the king's gate.
>
> (Esther 6:10)

Haman's balloon had burst. One can imagine his dismay
and anger!

School children love to mask themselves and paint color-ful faces in celebration of Purim, celebrating Esther's courage and victory over Haman.

The Second Banquet

The night of the second banquet came. Esther, Xerxes and Haman were there. Finally Queen Esther made her plea:

> If I have found favor in your sight...let my life be given me as my petition, and my people as my request;
>
> for we have been sold, I and my people, to be destroyed, to be killed and to be annihilated...
>
> (Esther 7:3-4)

Esther could have asked for and received half the Persian kingdom if she had selfish motives but instead she pleaded for the life of her people (Esther 7:2-4).

Xerxes, furious, asked who would persecute her people.

Esther pointed the finger at Haman.

Xerxes arose in anger and went into the palace garden. Haman stayed to beg for his life prostrating himself on the couch where Esther reclined.

Xerxes, returning, seeing Haman in this position, exclaimed:

> Will he even assault the queen with me in the house?
>
> (Esther 7:8)

Haman was then hung on the very gallows he had designed for the Jew, Mordecai. And Mordecai was made prime minister in Haman's place.

But the law of the Medes and the Persians could not be broken. Xerxes edict, issued under Haman's request, had to be carried out. The Jews, however, were allowed to unite in defense of their lives.

Victory At Last

On March 13, 473 B.C. the Jews slaughtered their enemies including Haman's 10 sons whose dead bodies were suspended from the gallows the next day.

This victory of the Jews over their enemies is celebrated as the Feast of Purim even today. Purim is so called because the word for "throwing dice" in Persian is "pur." And it was Haman's throwing of the dice to choose their death day that Jews through the ages remember in their celebration of thanks.

Xerxes was finally murdered by a servant in his royal court.

So, from the corruption of Xerxes to some 146 years later at 334 B.C., Persia had steadily declined as a potent power.

ENTER ALEXANDER

At this point Alexander was standing at the threshold anxious to include Persia in his kingdom!

Against Darius III, king of Persia, Alexander the Great moved his army of 40,000 men at the river Granicus. Some 20,000 Persians died. Only 115 men were lost by Alexander!

Meanwhile Darius III gathered 600,000 soldiers. It took five days just to march them over a bridge of boats across the Euphrates. And 600 mules and 300 camels were needed to carry the royal treasury!

Alexander met them at Issus, a small town that is now in south-central Turkey.

Darius III made the mistake of choosing a battlefield in which only a small amount of his army could fit. When the Persians retreated they had lost 110,000 men...Alexander, only 450. In fact Darius was so anxious to save his life he abandoned his mother, a wife, two daughters and his chariot!

The Tragedy Of Tyre

Alexander the Great then turned his armies toward Egypt. But first he desired to capture Tyre (now in present-day Lebanon). While at Tyre, Alexander received a message from Darius III suing for peace. Darius offered one of his daughters in marriage plus $300 million plus one-third of his empire...if Alexander would stop fighting.

Alexander refused!

Tyre did not give in easily. It took seven months of siege, 8000 Tyrians slain plus 2000 marched down to the sea and hanged! The remaining 30,000, including women and children, were sold into slavery. The date: July, 332 B.C.

Alexander the Great then reached Gaza. Gaza resisted but finally fell.

March Into Jerusalem

Jerusalem was the next goal. But the Jews and the Greeks had long been in business negotiations throughout the years—since 600 B.C.

In 334 B.C. Alexander the Great stood at the gates of Jerusalem and demanded the surrender of the capital. The high priest in the morning, having been warned by a dream which he said was from God, openly greeted Alexander and opened the city to him with great fanfare.

He ordered the priests to put on their most impressive garments. The people were told to wear an immaculate white garb. He then led the population out through the gates to solicit peace.

Alexander bowed to the high priest. He expressed his admiration for the people and their God, and entered Jerusalem in peace.

The Jews were split into two religious-political factions, one pro-Greek and one anti-Greek. The pro-Greek factions would compare to the "reform Jews" of today and the anti-Greek faction like the "orthodox Jews" of today.

Split Into 4 Kingdoms

Within 18 years of Alexander's death, his vast domain was ripped apart by four of his former generals.

> Antigonus grabbed Babylon and North Syria
> Ptolemy transformed Egypt into the Ptolemaic Empire
> Cassander took Macedonia (Northern Greece)
> Lysimachus seized Thrace and Bithynia (Northeastern
> Greece and N. Turkey)

Ten years later Seleucus I Nicator rises and soon has conquered Babylon, Syria, Thrace and Bithynia. Meanwhile Cassander is killed and loses Macedonia to Antigonus. Thus *FOUR* are still left.

It was to be a Seleucid king, Antiochus Epiphanes, who would bring great tragedy to the Jews in Jerusalem.

Alexander the Great, who had won an empire covering more than one and one-half million square miles, never realized that after his death it would be divided into four kingdoms: Greece, Turkey, Syria, and Egypt...thus fulfilling Daniel 8:22.

Palestine, laying between Syria and Egypt, would now become both the plum and the battleground over which these two Greek-ruled nations would fight.

It was the Romans who had been the first to call Alexander "the Great."

Sculptors in India created Buddha's image after the profile of Alexander the Great. Ethiopia made him a saint. Islam included him as a prophet.

In Daniel 11:2-3 it was prophesied:

> ...Behold, three more kings are going to arise in Persia. Then a fourth [that is, a fourth Persian king] will gain far more riches than all of them; as soon as he becomes strong through his riches, he will arouse the whole empire against the realm of Greece.

> And a mighty king will arise [that is, after the Persian kings], and he will rule with great authority and do as he pleases.

This "mighty king" was Alexander the Great! When Alexander came to the throne of Greece and Macedon he had only 40,000 soldiers and $75,000. The Persian king, Darius III had a yearly revenue of over $11 million, many millions in the treasury plus hundreds of thousands of soldiers and a great navy!

Yet, how true Daniel's prophecy became...for Alexander the Great (as noted in Daniel 11:3) did rise and with great authority and **he did do as he pleased!** Against overwhelming odds he crushed the Persian empire and empires beyond.

No More Worlds to Conquer

In 326 B.C. Alexander crossed the Indus, a river in South Asia flowing from West Tibet through Kashmir and Pakistan to the Arabian Sea. It was 1900 miles long.

It was at this river that Alexander, the hero, was found weeping

> ...because there were no more worlds to conquer.

Alexander, in one act, emulated David. It was in the Baluchistan desert...an arid mountainous region in southeast Iran and near Pakistan. The heat was unbearable. Soldiers had to butcher their transport animals for food and burn their baggage wagons for fuel. Finally, Alexander's scouts found a little water...just enough for **one** man. They brought it to their king. This was after 60 days of suffering on this burning desert.

Alexander Seeks an Oracle

Alexander was acclaimed as Pharaoh in Egypt and soon after he plunged into the Libyan Desert to query the Oracle of Ammon at Siwa Oasis. An Oracle is a supposedly divine utterance made by a god through a priest or priestess in response to an inquiry.

Alexander sought word of his future. From the inner sanctuary of the temple priests brought forth a golden bark bearing a ram-headed figure of the god Ammon. Ammon is an Egyptian deity whom the Greeks equated with Zeus. Alexander's mother claimed that Zeus had fathered Alexander. In the movements of the figure's head and body the priests read the answers to Alexander's questions.

This Thracian coin of the third century B.C. reflects Alexander's belief in his kinship with ram-horned Ammon.

And what did Alexander do? When offered a helmet of this precious water, while his men had none, he emptied it on the ground. In 2 Samuel 23:16 a similar example was made by King David.

Alexander's soldiers, tired of war, yearned to go back home. They refused to press on. Alexander yielded to the wishes of his men.

It must have been a magnificent scene...thousands of men marching down the river bank accompanied by a fleet of nearly 2000 vessels.

When Alexander arrived in Persepolis (ancient capital of Persia, now Iran), he found his new empire in disorder. The governors had exploited the people, overtaxing them and embezzling funds. He quickly executed the offenders. And to foster the union of East with West, he officiated at a ceremony where 10,000 of his troops married Persian women.

Despite the marriages, the Macedonians were determined not to be absorbed into the culture of Persia. Their resentment against their leader turned to hostility when they were next told that Alexander must be recognized as a god...the son of Zeus-Ammon, the supreme deity of the ancient Greeks.

When Alexander's dearest friend, Hephaestion, died, Alexander ordered a huge sepulcher to Hephaestion to be built in Babylon.

In 323 BC, Alexander arrived in Babylon to worship at this unfinished monument. He gave himself to sacrificing and drinking. One night he drained a huge goblet containing six quarts of wine.

When he died a reign of twelve years and eight months was ended. He had won an empire covering more than one and a half million square miles. He had mapped unknown territory. He had built cities, opened new trade routes.

Alexander's own words were:

> I set no limits of labors to a man of spirit, save only that the labors themselves...lead on to noble enterprises...It is a lovely thing to live with courage, and to die, leaving behind an everlasting renown.

But this man, whose power touched even Jerusalem, suddenly died almost like a drunkard, and his power quickly crumbled...for there was no one of stature to replace him. And it was part of this void that the terrible Antiochus IV Ephiphanes was to fill 150 years later...a name that would bring agony to the Jew.

7

ANTIOCHUS IV DESECRATES THE ALTAR

The entrance of Antiochus IV represents the bottom or fringed area of the copper skirt of the Greek Empire in the image of Daniel 2.

Daniel, in Daniel 11:4, foresaw what would occur after the reign of Alexander the Great:

> ...as soon as he [Alexander] has arisen, his kingdom will be broken up and parceled out toward the four points of the compass, though not to his own descendants, nor according to his authority which he wielded; for his sovereignty will be uprooted and given to others besides them.

It is interesting to note that in 15 years, not one of Alexander's family, including 3 wives, 2 sons, his brother and wife, and mother was left alive!

Thus, what was Alexander's alone, now was divided among 4 rulers...none of which was to achieve the power that Alexander enjoyed: Cassander to the west, Lysimachus to the north, Seleucus to the east, and Ptolemy to the south.

These four powers in a century of struggle eventually merged into two major powers

1. The Syrian division
   Ruled by the Seleucid line of kings

2. The Egyptian division
   Ruled by the Ptolemaic line of kings

It was from the Syrian-Seleucid line of kings that Antiochus IV was eventually to emerge. At first Seleucus I was one of Alexander's lesser generals...yet he boldy seized control of the northern part of Alexander's empire, about 312 B.C. He took the title Nicator...which means the Conqueror.

For his capital he chose a site near the aged Babylon, and the future Baghdad. It was to become his wealthiest city. After 35 years of popular rule, he was assassinated in 281 B.C.

The Rise of Antiochus IV

After various successors over the next 150 years, Antiochus IV gained the throne. It was custom that each ruler took a family name and a number and then added a complimentary additional name. Thus, the family name was

Antiochus
He was 4th in succession

And to his name and number he added the descriptive compliment

Epiphanes (which means Illustrious)

He was to become the most notorious and the most erratic ruler in his line. He allowed his delegates to abuse their power. And he gave his mistress authority over three cities.

He loved wine, women and art. It was said that he drank to excess and often left his royal seat at banquets, to dance naked with the entertainers.

He introduced the gladiatorial games in Antioch, his capital. He was so proud of his dubious accomplishments that he labeled his coins

Antochus Theos Epiphanes
(Antiochus, the God made Manifest)

Daniel also prophesied of the emergence of this powerful ruler who would bring tragedy to Jerusalem. In Daniel 8:8-9 we are told:

Then the male goat [Greece] magnified himself exceedingly. But as soon as he was mighty, the large horn [Alexander] was broken [he dies]; and in its place there came up four conspicuous horns [the 4 generals make themselves kings] towards the four winds of heaven.

And out of them [these 4 kingdoms] came forth a rather small horn [Antiochus IV Epiphanes] which grew exceeding great toward the south, toward the east, and toward the Beautiful Land [Palestine].

Antiochus IV was to rule from 175 to 164 B.C. Antiochus Epiphanes is often referred to as the antichrist of the Old Testament; and his deeds are a forerunner of what the real Antichrist will do during the last 3½ years of the Tribulation Period.

Some of Antiochus' enemies called him *Epimanes*...changing one letter in the Greek, a "ph" to an "m,"...which made the meaning "mad man." Antiochus was determined to break down Jewish tradition, and thus he encouraged the brother of a high priest, Jason, to build a gymnasium in Jerusalem.

On the surface this may appear to be a commendable thing. It, however, was part of a systematic program to convert the Jews to Greeks. Thus Jason, the High Priest, even preferred to use his Greek name rather than his Hebrew name of Joshua. And his goals were to introduce into Jerusalem Greek games and customs. This pleased Antiochus not only because it would make the Jews better Greeks, but also because it would add money to his coffers.

The Jews were not prejudiced against physical exercises but they objected to having young men and old alike running about in the open stark naked. The Second Book of Maccabees relates:

> ...the priests had no courage to serve any more at the altar, but despising the temple and neglecting the sacrifices, hastened to be partakers of the unlawful...

Some Jerusalem aristocrats were so eager to imitate the Greeks that—some writers said—they underwent operations to repair their circumcisions.

Antiochus' plan was beginning to work. The gymnasium changed the whole spiritual and social atmosphere of Jerusalem. In fact it began to rival the Temple as the social center.

Invasion of Egypt

In 170 B.C. the Egyptian king attempted to reconquer Palestine.

Antiochus, ruler of Palestine, not only stopped this invasion but chased the Egyptians back into their own country and

Under the direction of Antiochus, soldiers loot the Temple.

conquered them. Because he could not stay there personally, his grip of this country soon weakened and it became necessary for him to begin a second campaign against Egypt in 168 B.C.

This growing power by Antiochus worried Rome. The Roman Senate feared his military successes would threaten their existence. They issued orders demanding he leave Egypt. This brought about a very humiliating public encounter with the Roman envoy at Alexandria.

Antiochus asked the envoy for time to consider the Senate's directives. The envoy, Gaius Popilius Laenas, drew a circle around Antiochus and told him to:

> decide on the spot and not go out of that ring until
> he had given an answer to the Senate whether he
> would have peace or war with Rome.

Antiochus IV decided that the better side of discretion was to obey growing Rome.

The pride of Antiochus was devastated.

Previously Antiochus had attempted to Hellenize Palestine, that is, to make its people adopt Grecian customs.

Daniel foresaw that would happen in Daniel 8:10:

> And it [the little horn, Antiochus] grew up to the
> host of heaven and caused some of the host and
> some of the stars to fall to the earth, and it
> trampled them down.

What this verse means is that Antiochus would magnify
himself and even fight against the people of God and defeat
some of their leaders.

Verse 11 continues:

> It even magnified itself to be equal with the Com-
> mander of the host; and it removed the regular
> sacrifice from Him, and the place of His sanctuary
> was thrown down.

When a large number of Jews complained about Antiochus
IV unfair regulations, he simply had them put to death.
This passage in 1 Maccabees[1] gives us details on this
persecution:

> ...he [Antiochus IV Epiphanes] spake words of
> peace unto them, in deceit; and they gave him
> credence. And he fell suddenly upon the city,
> and smote it very sore, and destroyed much
> people of Israel. And when he had taken the spoils
> of the city, he set it on fire, and pulled down the
> houses and the walls thereof round about. And
> the women and the children took they captive,
> and took possession of the cattle (1:29-32).

Attack on Jerusalem

With Antiochus' pride damaged he decided to make sure
that Palestine was still loyal to him. This would provide
him with a buffer state between himself and the Romans.
His plan included sending his general Apollonius with
some 22,000 soldiers to Jerusalem on the Sabbath. They
came under the guise of peace and attacked on the Sab-

---

[1]First and Second Maccabees are two books relating to the events
centering around Judas the Maccabee and other heroes in the
Jewish struggle for political and religious freedom in the 2nd
century B.C. Scholars date 1 Maccabees at about 110 B.C. These
are not, however, part of the Bible.

Persecution under Antiochus IV. A priest, compelled to eat pork, prefers to die.

bath, knowing full well that orthodox Jews would not fight on that day.

Many people were killed. Women and children were taken as slaves. The city was sacked and burned.

Still not satisfied, in 167 B.C., Antiochus was determined at last to wipe out the Jewish religion. He forbade them to live in accordance with their ancestral laws.

He forbade them

1. To observe the Sabbath
2. To observe customary festivals
3. To observe traditional sacrifices

Circumcision was declared a crime. Women who chose to defy the royal edict by circumcising their sons were punished by the slaughter of their innocent circumcised child whose corpse was hung about its mother's neck. Remember, it was God Himself who ordered that all Jewish males were to be circumcized.

Jews were ordered to burn the Torah. They were forced to participate in pagan religious festivals. They were even forced to worship Zeus.

Beyond this, they were also forced to sing hymns to Bacchus, the god of wine; instead of to Jehovah.

Throughout all of Palestine they were compelled, under pain of death, to sacrifice to idols. And as a further desecration they were told not to kill a clean beast but rather a swine. Then to further humiliate them, they had to eat this unclean swine! Many brave Jews, rather than compromise, sacrificed themselves!

The Temple was given over to the worship of Olympian Zeus. His altar was erected in the entrance to the Temple and swine were sacrificed in his honor.

Some historians report that the Jews, as they fled this polluted city, cried out

"It is the abomination of desolation!"

This abomination of desolation occurred on December 16, 168 B.C. The final abomination is, however—as will be explained later—still future.

Antiochus IV Epiphanes got the surprise of his life. He did

not realize the zealousness of the orthodox Jew. He wanted to consolidate his empire, but this costly misjudgment sparked the Maccabean revolution (Daniel 11:32-35).

Antiochus, having troubles in Armenia and Persia, ordered Lysias (guardian of his son), to make an end to the Palestinian revolt and to destroy the Jews.

Obey or Die

So determined was Antiochus IV to have absolute rule that he sent forth an edict which in part stated:

> Let each man leave his laws and let all the nations accept the word of the king. And whoever does not carry out the king's request will be put to death.

Lysias, under the direction of Antiochus IV, dispatched a large army under the command of Ptolemy against the Jews who were led by Judas Maccabeus. Accompanying Ptolemy was an entourage of merchants who expected to purchase Jewish slaves in this conquest.

Judas brilliantly defeated the enemy at Emmaus, causing the Syrian soldiers to flee. Judas was a warrior whose courage equaled his dedication to the Lord. Before every battle he prayed, but in the hour of battle he was like a lion in his rage. Perhaps it was because he remembered the orgy of persecution imposed by Antiochus IV. Everywhere, Antiochus' agents had given the people a choice only between death and participation in Hellenic worship which included the eating of sacrificial swine. All synagogues and Jewish schools were closed.

On the drunken feast day of Bacchanalia [a festival in honor of Bacchus], Jews were compelled to deck themselves with ivy like the Greeks and sing wild songs in honor of Dionysus, the god of fertility and wine. Some Jews conformed. Most did not. Many Jews died because of their stand.

With this background, Judas was determined to fight like a lion. And like a lion he did fight. Not only did he turn the enemy back at Emmaus, but also at Mispah and finally Jerusalem. He removed all pagan altars from the Temple, cleansed and rededicated it and restored the holy rites. The Temple was rededicated three years after its desecration in December, 165 B.C. This is now celebrated as Hanukkah...the Jewish Feast of Lights.

This further angered Antiochus IV and he attempted an unsuccessful plundering of the temple of Nanaea/Artemis in Persia. He was able to escape, however, and died insane in Persia in 163 B.C.

There is no doubt that Antiochus IV Epiphanes was a type of the future Antichrist who will commit the final Abomination of Desolation. Matthew 24:15 proves this. These words of Christ, spoken 200 years *after* Antiochus committed his abomination, speak of yet another future Abomination of Desolation.

> *Therefore when you see the ABOMINATION OF DESOLATION which was spoken of through Daniel the prophet, standing in the holy place (let the reader understand)...*

He was a type in: (1) his persecution of the Jews and, (2) in his very proud attempt to exalt himself to a position of deity.

Antiochus brought a temporary end to the sacrifices just as Antichrist will bring an end to the sacrifices in the Tribulation Period.

Both Antiochus and Antichrist are involved in placing an ungodly image in the Temple.

> And he deceives those who dwell on the earth because of the signs which it was given him to perform in the presence of the beast, telling those who dwell on the earth to make an image to the beast who had the wound of the sword and has come to life (Revelation 13:14).

It is interesting to note Daniel's revelation of Daniel 7:25:

> *And he [Antichrist] will speak out against the Most High and wear down the saints of the Highest One, and he will intend to make alterations in times and in law...*

Notice that both Alexander the Great and Antiochus IV Epiphanes were prototypes of this reform plan.

Alexander's strategy was to populate Palestine with Greek soldiers. He also encouraged mixed marriages. He strove

There appears to be a resurgence of persecution against
the Jews today. Roberta Savitsky cries unconsolably as her
father Rabbi Mordecai Savitsky lifts badly damaged Torah
from the Holy Ark in Boston synagogue. Vandals set fire to
sacred scroll, smashed windows.

to achieve an empire with a common language, custom and culture.

Antiochus, on the other hand, introduced pagan rites into Palestine and sought to eliminate Jewish observances and sacrifices.

As Antiochus suffered opposition of his tyranny, so Antichrist will face the opposition of the 144,000 Jews during the Tribulation Period.

Here's another interesting fact:

> When Antiochus IV invaded Egypt for the second time, a rumor spread all over his kingdom that he had been killed in Egypt. When Antiochus heard this he was furious and returned to slaughter thousands of Jews.

We are also told three times in Revelation 13 that Antichrist had a death wound that was healed. Then we know that after this much persecution is imposed on the believers (Revelation 13:3,12,14 and 7).

While Antiochus IV today is just another name in history... the people he sought to persecute continue with their sacred customs even up to today. And, through Hannakuh, Antiochus, by no design of his own, has further strengthened the Jewish cause by another festival of ultimate victory over persecution by God's help!

8

THE JEWISH STRUGGLE AGAINST ROME
Pompey the Great Invades Jerusalem

When Pompey, the Roman general, entered the Jewish Temple in Jerusalem in 63 BC, it signaled the end of the Jews' brief century of independence and ushered in another historic era of suffering for the Jewish nation.

Jerusalem at this time was a city where many of its streets were paved with marble...a city of some 600,000 population.

The mass of its inhabitants were living in poverty but there were a large number of wealthy people. The sources of the income of this minority were:

(1) Estates
(2) Trade
(3) Sacrifices, offerings, and Temple dues (half-shekel tax from every Jew in Palestine)

Many of the rich were, of course, priestly families. Some of the rich acted as tax collectors for the Romans. This made them very unpopular. It was said, perhaps in jest, that the daughter of one rich man received such a large allowance for her perfumes...that the money could have supplied the whole country with food for ten years (Midrash I.48).

The Midrash, a series of historic Jewish books, tells of the many banquets held in Jerusalem. No one would accept an invitation to a banquet unless invited twice and unless he knew who else was invited.

The relative peace that the Jewish people were enjoying was soon to be cut short with the entrance of Pompey...a struggle that would begin at 63 BC and continue to 73 AD... some 100 years!

In the image of Daniel 2, this represented the upper portion of the iron legs, Roman the Republic and Empire.

Pompey was a Roman general (106-48 BC), one of a triumvirate who was to control Rome. The other two of the "big three" were Julius Caesar and Crassus, Rome's richest man. It was the cruel Crassus who hung rebels of Rome on crosses along the Appian Way.

This triumvirate created an army of calloused soldiers... some say the greatest army in history. Caesar wooed his men by doubling their pay, sharing spoils and winking at their off-duty escapades. He once remarked:

My men fight just as well stinking of perfume.

But he hated cowards. He even at times had every tenth man in a cowardly unit slain, as an example for others.

It was not long until Rome spread her mighty empire from Britain's northern snows to the sands of Syria. Not only did Caesar invade Britain but he met and mastered Cleopatra in Alexandria.

Pompey, born in Rome, was the last obstacle in Julius Caesar's rise to power. The very fact that Caesar gave his daughter Julia to Pompey in marriage proved the only link that kept the two leaders from open conflict.

It was said that Pompey the Great was sensitive and shy and that he blushed when he had to address a public gathering. Perhaps his outstanding fault was vanity. He wondered when Rome would make him King. Pompey's strength grew when the Assembly at Rome voted him an army of 125,000 men and a navy of 500 vessels and ordered the Treasury to place over $5 million at his disposal.

Meanwhile Palestine was governed by the Hasmoneon dynasty. This was the name applied to the descendants of Simon, the last surviving brother of Judas Maccabeus, the leader of the revolt against Antiochus IV.

Sacrilege and Massacre

At the time of Pompey's power, Alexander Jannaeus was ruling Palestine. Jannaeus, a Hasmoneon, ruled a territory that covered not only Palestine but also the area now known as Jordan and parts of Egypt.

Jannaeus and the Pharisees were at odds with each other. And the straw that broke the camel's back was when Jannaeus poured out the sacramental wine at his own feet instead of on the altar. The people were so angry they pelted him with oranges and grapefruits. Jannaeus retaliated by killing 6000 people (Josephus, *Antiquities,* 13:13:5).

It was reported that Jannaeus had 800 Jewish rebels crucified in a single day. As they hung, dying slowly, on the crosses, it is said that he let them watch their wives and children being butchered below while he himself, reclining at ease and drinking wine.[1]

When Jannaeus died, his two sons, Hyrcanus and Aristobulus, sought to take control of Israel. This was complicated by Antipater, an Arab from Jordan, also seeking control. All three sought favors from the Roman general Pompey, who had conquered the area.

Aristobulus, although successful in becoming King of Palestine, offered to surrender Jerusalem to Pompey.

But when Pompey's courier went to Jerusalem to collect money, Aristobulus' zealous supporters would not let the courier into the city.

This action enraged Pompey and he made King Aristobulus a prisoner.

Turmoil ensued in Jerusalem. Supporters of the King wanted to fight. Others wanted to surrender to Pompey. The Pompey supporters in Jerusalem chased their opponents into the Temple, then opened the gates of the city to welcome the Roman General. But with Pompey's entrance the fight was not yet over!

It took three months to overcome the resisters because there was a valley and a great ditch adjacent to the Temple. This had to be filled in with soil. Pompey, knowing the Jews would not fight on the Sabbath, used this day to fill the ditch.

Pompey was amazed that even as the Temple was being captured and Jews were being butchered...still the faithful did not abandon their ceremonies. Many of the priests, Josephus reports, though they saw the enemy approaching sword in hand, quietly went on with the sacred rites and were murdered as they were pouring out the sacramental libations on the altar.

---

[1]George C. Brauer, Jr., *Judea Weeping*, New York: Corwell, 1970, p. 13.

That day the Jews lost 12,000 dead. This occurred in 63 BC.

Pompey then went into the Holy of Holies inside the Sanctuary, which no one was permitted to enter but the high priest. He saw the lampstand, the lamps, the table, the libation cups and the censers...all solid gold plus a great quantity of spices and sacred money, totaling in value some $10 million.

However, he did not lay a finger on any of this. And only one day after the capture he instructed the custodians to purify the Temple and perform the normal sacrifices.

Titus burns the Temple in Jerusalem. Of the destruction, Tacitus said: "They cause desolation to reign and call it peace." Many of the survivors were taken to Rome where they were either sold as slaves, thrown to the wild beasts in the arenas, or thrown from the Tarpeian Rock for the amusement of the crowds.

Later, Pompey fearful of Caesar's ever-growing power, fought him in a series of battles. When Pompey fled to Egypt he was stabbed to death as he stepped from his ship.

Pompey the Great, conquerer of Jerusalem, suddenly in an instant met his end at the hands of one of his own countrymen!

TITUS, Invader of Jerusalem

It was the year 64 AD. Nero was emperor of Rome. He had just appointed Gessius Florus as the new procurator to Judaea.

Florus was not a popular man among the Jews. He showed himself to be the most heartless of men. He stripped whole cities and wanted to drive the Jews to revolt. In one fit of anger Florus had his troops kill 3,360 Jews.

He tried to force Jews out of Jerusalem so he could steal the treasures of the Temple.

The Jews begged Agrippa II to send letters and ambassadors to Rome to demand that Florus be removed. It was this Agrippa of whom it was said that he lived in incest with his sister, Berenice.

Faced with these troubles, Agrippa II, descendant of Herod the Great, called together the Jewish leaders in an attempt to appease them. Realizing they wanted to go to war against Rome, he questioned them saying:

> Where are the men, where are the weapons you can count on? Where is the fleet that is to sweep the Roman seas? Where are the funds to pay for your expeditions? Do you think you are going to war with Egyptians and Arabs?

> Consider the defences of the Britons, you who feel so sure of the defences of Jerusalem. They were surrounded by the Ocean and inhabit an island as big as this continent; yet the Romans crossed the sea and enslaved them, and four legions keep that huge island.

> Almost every nation under the sun bows down before the might of Rome; and will you alone go to war, not even considering the fate of the Carthaginians...

So there is no refuge left except to make God your ally. But He too is ranged on the Roman side, for without His help so vast an empire could never have been built up.

...if you make a right decision you will share with me the blessings of peace, but if you are carried away by your passions you will go without me to your doom.

(Josephus, the Wars of the Jews)

But the people would not listen.

And in the interim some zealots captured Masada and exterminated the Roman garrison there. Then a civil war broke out in Jerusalem between those loyal to Agrippa II and those seeking freedom from Rome's domination.

Hearing of the massacre of their 300 soldiers in Jerusalem... the Romans killed and allowed to be killed some 20,000 Jews in Caesaraea. The Romans then began a systematic punishment of Galilee. Over 6000 youths were sent to Nero to work on the canal at Corinth; 1200 old men were killed and another 30,000 Jews were sold as slaves.

Then Cestius Gallus, Roman governor of Syria, tried to quell the revolt in Jerusalem, only to meet defeat.

Rome had been insulted...but not defeated. And the road ahead for the Jews was to be one of bitter consequences.

The Rise of NERO

Nero, the tyrant of Rome, at the time was on a musical and dramatic tour of Greece. He was 29. His accomplishments? He had:

1. Ordered the assassination of his mother;
2. Murdered his rich aunt;
3. Ordered his teacher, Seneca, to commit suicide;
4. And it was reported, raped boys and girls in public.

Nero, hearing of the revolt, ordered his general, Vespasian, to quell the revolt.

Vespasian sent his son Titus to Alexandria to pick up a legion of men, while he assembled his army at Antioch in Syria. He then met his son with a total combined army of some 58,000 men.

Christian and Jew alike were killed in Rome.

One can almost picture this sight...cavalry units with each rider having a sword handy at his right side, a long spear in his hand; heavily armed Roman soldiers with big, oblong shields gleaming in the sunshine. Each group of a thousand men was preceded by an honor guard bearing the golden eagle of Rome...a symbol the Jews despised.

When Nero died in the interim...rivals sought to become Emperor of Rome. Vespasian succeeded in 70 AD.

TITUS...Destroyer of Jerusalem

Busy with the affairs at Rome, Vespasian dispatched his son, Titus, to the task of ending the revolt of the Jews.

The actual siege of Jerusalem began in the autumn of 69AD. In the spring of 70, Titus took over command of the Roman troops. It did not take long for the Roman army to smash the outer northern wall of Jerusalem.

Titus next attacked the middle wall. This, too, was conquered.

All that remained was the most critical wall: the one extending from Herod's old palace on the west to the Temple hill on the east. This protected a major area of Jerusalem. Here within also was the Temple.

To capture this last stronghold the Romans prepared their most strategic offenses. The Jews, in defense, had built 40 machines for firing stones and three hundred for firing arrows.

The city was now beset by famine.

Some Jews, so desperate, tried to sneak into the Roman occupied part of the city to hunt for food and then return to the Temple area.

Other Jews swallowed gold pieces, and attempted to escape from the beseiged Jerusalem during Titus' attack. The savage Parthians, Roman allies on the scene, capturing them, slit open their bellies to find the coins.

500 Jews Crucified Daily

Many were caught daily. Titus decided to impress on them the severity of Roman punishment. The historian Josephus says that 500 or more Jews were crucified daily, in plain view of the citizens defending the wall.

Titus finally decided the only way to conquer Jerusalem was to surround it with his own siege wall.

The famine got so bad that many were gnawing their leather belts and shoes and swallowing dry grass.

Finally, one day the Roman soldiers succeeded in gaining access to the Temple area. Josephus says that one zealous soldier seized a piece of wood from one of the outer gates which had been set on fire, ran with it, and tossed it directly into the very Sanctuary itself.

Titus ran from his tent to witness the Temple going up in flames. The scene excited the Roman soldiers to a frenzy. They killed the Jews and heaped their bodies on the terrace on which the marble Sanctuary stood and around the rough Altar of Burnt Offerings in the court below.

They grabbed the treasures and plundered the Temple of every element of intrinsic value.

Below, in the city the Jews gazed up at their burning Temple. God had abandoned Jerusalem. No longer were

Titus executed the leaders of the Jewish revolt.

there gates of bronze and silver nor the veil of four colors, nor the massed treasures. There would be no more high priest, no more morning and evening sacrifices. The angry red flames crackled out defeat and the spiralling black clouds sent the signal to the watching countryside.

Titus executed the leaders of the Jewish revolt. The rest were sent in chains to Egypt to labor in the mines or to be sold in Rome as slaves. Some were to be unwilling combatants in gladiatorial combats being pitted against beasts.

Titus then ordered Jerusalem to be leveled to the ground. So fell Jerusalem in the second year of Vespasian's reign, on the 9th of **Ab** (August 28th), 70 AD. It had been captured five times before...and now, for the second time, was laid utterly waste.

Shishak, king of Egypt, followed by Antiochus IV, then Pompey, Sossius and Herod—all captured the City but spared it.

But the king of Babylon destroyed it...as did Titus again 7 centuries later.

Even today at weddings, in the midst of their joy, Jewish bridegrooms crush a glass beneath their heel to recall the Temple's destruction.

Titus was not to be Emperor of Rome long. He died in his second year of rule in 81 AD.

HADRIAN...Suppressor of the Jews

Publius Aelius Hadrianus, better known as Hadrian, became Emperor of Rome in 117 AD. Perhaps Hadrian's most famous construction was the Pantheon in Rome; a temple for Roman gods.

One of his first actions was to cancel the taxes of those who were behind in their payment. The cancellation amounted to some $3 1/2 billion!

In 130 AD he journeyed to Jerusalem. The Holy City was still in ruins, almost as Titus had left it 60 years before. Hadrian, perhaps touched by its desolation, ordered that Jerusalem be rebuilt as a Roman colony and renamed, Aelia Capitolina.

The rebuilding of Jerusalem into a pagan city angered many Jews.

Hadrian, determined to keep the Jews from gaining new strength, forbade not only circumcision (which he considered barbaric) but also the observance of the Sabbath or any Jewish holiday. He placed a new and heavier poll tax upon all Jews. They were allowed in Jerusalem only on one fixed day each year, when they might come and weep before the ruins of their Temple.

In what was once their Holy City, Jews now saw shrines to Jupiter and Venus.

The Jews remembered that it was Hadrian who went to Egypt, enticed the Jews of Alexandria into the open country and then gave the order for about 50,000 of them to be massacred.

To lead the Jews, a zealot fighter by the name of Bar Kokhbah became the Messianic standard bearer of his people. The Second Jewish Revolt had begun (132-134 AD). The Romans after two years finally quelled this rebellion and he was killed. What was left of the Temple site was plowed over and the pagan city of Aelia Capitolina became a reality.

Thousands of Jews lost their lives and almost a thousand villages were razed in Judea. By the time this war was finished Hadrian had succeeded in completely destroying Jerusalem and making Judea a defoliated desert. Olives, one of the country's main crops, were not harvested again for more than 100 years! The Romans had won another war!

To eradicate the stubborn nationalism of the Jews, the name of the province of Judea was changed to Paletina, after the Jews' ancient adversaries, the Philistines.

To divide the city into neat quarters, the Romans laid out two wide colonnaded main streets that intersected at Jerusalem's exact center (still discernible today). Looking down from above, it would appear as though a great cross had been placed over the city.

At Golgotha, where Jesus was crucified, Hadrian erected temples dedicated to Venus, Jupiter and other gods.

Over the site of the Temple of Solomon, Hadrian erected a gate with the carving of a swine. No Jew was permitted to enter the city. Any who did enter would be crucified... except for the one day of the year specified by Roman law.

Aelia, as a pagan city, remained a small provincial garrison town.

Eighteen centuries were to pass before the Jews could regain control over the land that Jehovah had once given to their ancestors!

9

THE UNHOLY CRUSADES

The advent of the Crusades was perhaps the most tragic movement of the medieval period.

The medieval period, often known as the Middle Ages or Dark Ages, covers a period of world history from 400 AD to 1400 AD.

What brought about the movement of the Crusades?

There were perhaps four reasons:

1. In 1070 AD the Turks had taken Jerusalem from the Fatimids of Egypt. The Turks soon began to desecrate the holy sites and oppress the pilgrims in the city.

2. The Eastern Roman Empire, with Constantinople as its capital, was beginning to crumble.

3. Several Italian cities desired to extend their rising commercial power and hoped to override growing Moslem power in the Mediterranean.

4. Urban II, an ambitious Pope, had visions of once again bringing the Eastern church under papal rule...making Rome the capital of the world.

In an impassioned plea this French Pope, on a cold November day, told his countrymen:

> ...Enter upon the road to the Holy Sepulcher; wrest that land from a wicked race, and subject it to yourselves...That royal city, situated at the center of the earth, implores you to come to her aid. Undertake this journey eagerly for the remission of your sins and be assured of the reward of imperishable glory in the Kingdom of Heaven.

By March, 1096 AD the first crusade was on its way to Jerusalem. Their combined armies totaled over 30,000. By the time they reached the walls of Jerusalem three years later on June 7, 1099 this army had been reduced to some 12,000 combatants.

CRUSADERS MASSACRE ARABS

The Crusaders' report of the results of their assault reads something like a modern day war memo:

> Wonderful things were to be seen. Numbers of the Saracens [Arabs] were beheaded...others were shot with arrows, or forced to jump from the towers; others were tortured for several days and then burned in flames. In the streets were seen piles of heads and hands and feet. One rode about everywhere amid the corpses of men and horses.

Some 70,000 Moslems who remained in the city of Jerusalem were slaughtered. The surviving Jews were herded into a synagogue and then burned alive.

It seemed that Crusaders could not distinguish between the Arab armies and the Jew. Both suffered the same fate at the hand of the cross-breasted Crusaders who came to save Jerusalem for Christianity.

There were three other chief Crusades along with some minor ones, and all finally ended in failure in 1291 AD.

While Mohammed had confiscated the wealth of the Jews in the 600's AD...because they would not join him in his battle against the "pagans," after Mohammed died, Arab and Jew lived in relative peace for over 500 years.

But the Crusades had changed all that.

ARABS RETALIATE

The Moslem powers, angered by the attacks of the Crusaders, suddenly became fiercely intolerant of other religions. Not only Jews, but also Christians were now to suffer persecution in the years to come.

Jews, for the most part, had enjoyed a harassed prosperity from the eighth to the twelfth century. Under a Moslem Spain the Spanish Jews enjoyed some 300 years of relative freedom. But with a sudden change in power in 1066 the Arabs massacred 4000 Jews in Granada and plundered their homes. The honeymoon was over.

A Mohammedan theologian reported that the Jews had promised Mohammed to accept Islam at the end of the 500 year period commemmorating the flight of Mohammad from Mecca to Medina in 622 AD, if by that time their expected Messiah had not come. The Moslem ruler demanded they either convert to Islam or pay an enormous sum into the treasury.

Continued harrassment of the Jew went on for centuries in Spain which included the Papal-backed forcing Jews to wear a yellow identification badge, the segregation of Jews from the Christian population and the banning of the employment of Jewish physicians by Christians.

Similar decrees of badge identification, sponsored always by "the Church," were enforced in England in 1218, in France in 1219, and in Hungary in 1279.

In 1235 AD an unsolved murder in Germany was laid to the Jews. A massacre of the Jews ensued. Then in 1243 the entire Jewish population of Belitz, near Berlin, was burned alive. This rampage continued on and off, and in 1298 every Jew in Röttingen was burned to death on the charge of descrating a sacramental wafer!

The persecutions continued to spread and withing a half a year after this incident over 140 Jewish congregations were wiped out.

In 1144 when young William of Norwich of England was found dead, Jews were blamed. It was Jews who were among those who had loaned money to the Crusaders to finance their years of terror. (This was, of course, because "the Church" forbade Christians to loan money at usury, i.e., interest.) Now with the Crusaders home they resented the wealth of many of the Jews. This resentment built up between 1257 and 1267, and the populace got out of hand. Edward I ordered the remaining Jews in England to leave the country. Many were drowned in crossing the Channel.

When they reached France, they sought to rebuild their lives...only to find...after they had done so...that Philip the Fair (1306) had them all imprisoned. Then he took everything they had except the clothes on their backs and expelled the 100,000 Jews from France with only enough food for one day.

In 1235 AD an unsolved murder in Germany was laid to the Jews. A massacre of the Jews ensued.

So the Jew was to wander down through the Middle Ages... hated and despised seeking each time anew a peaceful spot to place his weary foot—only to find the ground give way to bury him once again in tragedy.

Perhaps it was at this time that the seeds of a desire for a permanent home again built up in the breasts of Jews.

One who lived during this time, Solomon Ibn Gabirol, who lost both parents early in life and grew up in poverty, wrote:

> We wander ever to and fro,
>   Or sit in chains in exile drear;
> Yet still proclaim, where'er we go,
>   The splendor of our Lord is here.

And Jehuda Halevi, considered at that time the greatest European poet of his age, penned:

> O City of the World [Jerusalem], beauteous in proud
>   splendor!
> Oh, that I had eagle's wings that I might fly to thee,
> Till I wet thy dust with my tears!
> My heart is in the East, while I tarry in the West.

10

THE HITLER YEARS...
PRELUDE TO THE GREAT TRIBULATION

At half past six on the evening of April 20, 1889, a baby boy was born in an inn in the small town of Braunau in Bavaria.

His name...Adolf Hitler. It was a name that was to bring terror and death to millions of European Jews!

It seems odd that Hitler's initial ambition was to enter the Academy of Fine Arts in Vienna to become an architect. He failed to pass the test and spent five obscure years as a casual laborer and amateur painter.

He learned how to fake paintings of the masters, roast them in an oven until they had become quite brown and aged looking.

In Vienna as early as 1911 he started to acquire an ingrained hatred for the Jews. Anti-semitism in this city was having its roots that soon would engulf the whole world. Hitler already at this time believed there was a Jewish world conspiracy to destroy and subdue the Aryan peoples. He believed the Jew responsible for modernism in art and music, pornography and prostitution, and the exploitation of the masses.

Hitler's Rise To Power

After World War I with the overthrow of the German Empire a void was created of unrest. Adolf Hitler, through a series of odd circumstances, was destined to fill that void. He joined the German Worker's Party and soon learned the art of propaganda. His propaganda lessons included the following:

> The receptive powers of the masses are very restricted, and their understanding is feeble... they quickly forget.

> When you lie, tell big lies.

By 1930 Hitler and his National Socialist (Nazi) party had gradually risen to become a major factor in national politics. The Government was deeply in debt, farmers and workers were desperate, hard pressed to pay the interest on mortgages and loans...they were seeing their homes being forfeited...more than 6 million were unemployed!

Through a series of clever maneuvers by the Nazi Party Hindenburg was convinced against his will that the only salvation for Germany lay in his appointing Adolf Hitler as Chancellor. This he did on January 30, 1933.

The army saw in Hitler the man who promised to restore Germany's military power. Industrialists saw Hitler as the man who would defend their interests against the threat of Communism. The masses saw in Hitler someone who, at last, claimed that he had the answers—not only to save Germany from economic chaos, but also to make her great again.

Hitler, alert for all angles, saw how the people feared the spectre of communism. Anxious to gain complete control over Germany, Hitler created a decree which he had signed by the unsuspecting Hindenburg "for the protection of the People and the State."

The decree was described "as a defensive measure against Communist acts of violence."

Hitler Masters The Big Lie

It suspended the guarantees of individual liberty under the Weimar Constitution. It was the first step to give Hitler full power!

On March 4, Hitler gave a fiery speech commemmorating this action:

> German people, hold your heads high and proudly once more! You are no longer enslaved and in bondage, but you are free again and can justly say: We are all proud that through God's powerful aid we have once more become true Germans.

Even Hitler knew when to usher in God's name when it could be used to his advantage. What a paradox! The Germans had just had their freedoms taken away from them with Hitler's decree and yet his speech tells them to hold their heads high because they are no longer enslaved!

Once again Hitler had mastered the technique of the Big Lie!

Adolf Hitler in mass rally in 1934.

Hitler finally became Dictator of Germany on a single law known as the Enabling Law. This law gave the Government the power for four years to enact laws without the cooperation of the Reichstag [the lower house of the German parliament].

This gave Hitler power to deviate from the Constitution and to conclude treaties with foreign states. Hitler moved fast doing just the things no one believed he would do...he banned all opposition parties...and everyone was so shocked that no one dared to stand against these acts. Goering and Himmler, his aides, had done well their preparatory work of propaganda and terror.

Hitler had little love for the Protestant clergy. He remarked:

> They are insignificant little people, submissive as dogs, and they sweat with embarrassment when you talk to them. They have neither a religion they can take seriously nor a great position to defend like Rome.

Hitler also said:

> The Jew has never founded any civilization, though he has destroyed hundreds. He possesses nothing of his own creation to which he can point. Everything he has stolen.

Hitler's hatred for the Jew was so intense that six million Jews were to perish in Eastern and Western Europe under his rule!

Hitler's Systematic Terror Against Jews

The first system of terror instituted by Hitler was through the Gestapo, organized by Hermann Goering.

Eventually a chicken farmer and fertilizer salesman by the name of Heinrich Himmler took over the powerful S.S. (Secret State Police).

By the end of 1933 there were 50 concentration camps. Himmler's S.S. absorbed the Gestapo into one unified police force.

The first blow to the Jews came through the passage of the Nuremberg Laws in September, 1935. This deprived the Jews of German citizenship. A further law forbade marriage and sexual relations between Jews and Germans and imposed heavy penalties. By 1937 the situation became unbearable. The Jew could not vote, he could not defend himself in print. He could not work as a writer, artist or musician. He was denied food and drugs in certain stores.

In 1937, 23,000 Jews left Germany. This brought the total number who had left since 1933 to 129,000. This represented about one fourth of the Jewish population in Germany in 1933. By 1938 it became almost impossible for a Jew to leave Germany.

On June 9, 1938 Hitler's first bold move was the destroying of the Great Synagogue in Munich. Soon other synagogues were destroyed. In 1938 Hitler's aides tried various means of coercion to make the Jews flee Germany, but by 1942 they sought only to exterminate them.

Under the direction of Adolf Eichmann, Reinhard Heydrich, Heinrich Himmler and others...plans were made to both utilize Jewish labor and to destroy those considered unuseable in the cause.

Who can forget the tragedy that lurked in the concentration camps of Auschwitz, Belsen, Buchenwald, Ravensbruck and others!

Such books as The Diary of Anne Frank and The Hiding Place by Corrie ten Boom graphically described the pathos and the hopelessness of the era as well as the intense suffering and death. And today, thousands of Jews still bear the tattooed serial number which was once indelibly etched on the their arm in a concentration camp.

Yet although these events of terror occurred less than 50 years ago, with millions killed in gas chambers and ovens, already most of us have all but forgotten the curious play of events that made this possible.

The Greatest Tragedy

What is perhaps the most amazing fact to comprehend is that while all this mass slaughter was going on, most nations either looked on indifferently or for the sake of expedience, pretended not to notice it.

Perhaps a document, which stands as one of the most terrifying in all the literature of his holocaust, was written by a German civilian construction engineer on October 5, 1942.

This man was a witness to the annihilation of the Dubno Ghetto in the Ukraine.

He wrote:

About 1500 persons had been killed daily. There were about 5000 more Jews yet to be killed. Armed Ukrainian militia drove the people off the trucks under the supervision of an S.S. man. All these people had the regulation yellow patches on the front and back of their clothes, and thus could be recognized as Jews.

The people who had got off the trucks — men, women and children of all ages — had to undress upon the order of an S.S. man who carried a dog whip. They had to put down their clothes in fixed places, sorted according to shoes, top clothing and underclothing. I saw a heap of shoes of about 800 to 1000 pairs.

Without screaming or weeping these people undressed, stood around in family groups, kissed each other, said farewells and waited for a sign from another S.S. man, who stood near the pit, also with a whip in his hand.

During the 15 minutes that I stood near the pit, I heard no complaint or plea for mercy. An old woman with snow-white hair was holding the one-year old child in her arms and singing to it and tickling it. The couple were looking on with tears in their eyes. The father was holding the hand of a boy about 10 years old and speaking to him softly; the boy was fighting back his tears. The father pointed to the sky.

At that moment, the S.S. man at the pit shouted something to his comrade. The latter counted off about 20 persons and instructed them to go behind the earth mound. Among them was the family I have mentioned.

I walked around the mound and found myself confronted by a tremendous grave. People were closely wedged together and lying on top of each other so that only their heads were visible. Nearly all had blood running over their shoulders from

I looked for the man who did the shooting...he had a tommy gun on his knees and he was smoking a cigarette.

their heads. Some of the people shot were still moving. Some were lifting up their arms and turning their heads to show that they were still alive. The pit was already two-thirds full. I estimated that it already contained about a thousand people.

I looked for the man who did the shooting. He was an S.S. man, who sat at the edge of the narrow end of the pit, his feet dangling into the pit. He had a tommy gun on his knees and he was smoking a cigarette.

The people, completely naked, went down some steps which were cut in the clay wall of the pit and clambered over the heads of the people lying there, to the place where the S.S. man directed them. They lay down in front of the dead or injured people; some caressed those who were still alive and spoke to them in a low voice.

Then I heard a series of shots.

I looked into the pit and saw that the bodies were twitching. Blood was running from their necks. The next batch was approaching already. They went down into the pit, lined themselves up against the previous victims and were shot.

When I walked back, I noticed another truckload of people which had just arrived. This time it included sick and infirm. An old, very thin women with terribly thin legs was undressed by others who were already naked, while two people held her up.

When the British troops captured the area where the Belsen concentration camp was located they found 28,000 women, 12,000 men and 13,000 unburied corpses. Within a few days 13,000 more died of malnutrition. Yet just two miles away in the larders of the German army school were stored 800 tons of food and a bakery that had the capacity to produce 60,000 loaves of bread a day!

In April, 1945 Adolf Hitler along with his mistress, Eva Braun, were found burned to death in a Berlin bunker. The German dream had become a nightmare! It became a nightmare not only for the Jews, but also for millions of Germans who also reaped suffering from the bombs falling from above and from the invading Russians from the east.

Europe in the twelve years between 1933 and 1945 had become a vast cemetery of Jews whose remains were ashes in unnamed graves.

Six million Jews brutally killed...but the world has soon forgotten. Some even today still praise this accomplishment of the German Reich.

Except for God's intervention, the Hitler years are but a prelude to the awesome tragedy from Satan's hand that awaits the Jew in the Great Tribulation.

Henry Kissinger at cocktail party after his talks in Jerusalem. (l. to r.) Minister of Immigration, Prime Minister Rabin, Henry Kissinger, Dinnitz (with back) and Yigal Allon.

11

THE RISE OF ISRAEL'S MOST VICIOUS PERSECUTOR

Three top Israeli leaders and Secretary of State Henry A. Kissinger faced each other behind the closed doors of the prime minister's office in Jerusalem.

The time was late Saturday night, March 22, 1975.

Yigal Allon, Israeli Foreign Minister, turned to Kissinger to say that he expected the secretary back in the Middle East in two or three weeks.

Allon was an old friend of Kissinger. And it was in sadness that Henry Kissinger had to tell his friend that this peace mission had failed. In fact, personal shuttle diplomacy seemed to have reached an end...the negotiations between Israel and Egypt had been shattered!

Later that same evening, in the privacy of Kissinger's King David hotel room, Shimon Peres, Israeli Defense Minister, broke down into tears.

It was a dramatic moment when the full weight of the consequences hit these leaders as they realized that the failure of this mission again meant an uncertain future for the Middle East.

At the airport, Henry Kissinger held back the tears. His voice trembled as he said that it was a sad day for Israel and for the United States.

Henry Kissinger had staked his reputation and that of the United States on this two-week shuttle diplomacy. His mistake was in believing he could move either Egypt or Israel from a standstill position.

Anwar Sadat, the Egyptian President, was not willing to meet certain Israeli demands. And the Israeli's were not willing to cede territorial conquests.

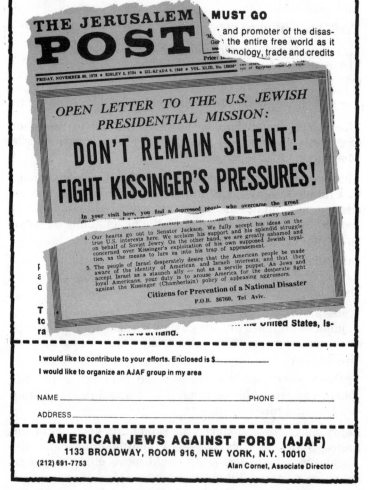

For the sake of the United States, the free world and Israel

PRESIDENT FORD MUST GO

With respect and honor for the office of the Presidency but with a terrible sense of fear for the future of the United States and the free world, we call for a change in administration in 1976.

THE JERUSALEM POST

... MUST GO

... and promoter of the disas-
... the entire free world as it
...hnology, trade and credits

FRIDAY, NOVEMBER 30, 1973 • KISLEV 5, 5734 • EIL-KI'ADA 6, 1393 • VOL. XLIII, No. 13056 •

OPEN LETTER TO THE U.S. JEWISH PRESIDENTIAL MISSION:

DON'T REMAIN SILENT!
FIGHT KISSINGER'S PRESSURES!

In your visit here, you find a depressed people who overcame the great
...

4. Our hearts go out to Senator Jackson. We fully accept his ideas on the true U.S. interests here. We acclaim his support and his splendid struggle on behalf of Soviet Jewry. On the other hand, we are greatly ashamed and concerned over Kissinger's exploitation of his own supposed Jewish loyalties, as the means to lure us into his trap of appeasement.

5. The people of Israel desperately desire that the American people be made aware of the identity of American and Israeli interests, and that they accept Israel as a staunch ally — not as a servile puppet. As Jews and loyal Americans, your duty is to arouse America for the desperate fight against the Kissinger (Chamberlain) policy of appeasing aggressors.

Citizens for Prevention of a National Disaster
P.O.B. 36760, Tel Aviv.

... United States, Is-

... is at hand.

- -

I would like to contribute to your efforts. Enclosed is $_____

I would like to organize an AJAF group in my area

NAME _____ PHONE _____

ADDRESS _____

- -

AMERICAN JEWS AGAINST FORD (AJAF)
1133 BROADWAY, ROOM 916, NEW YORK, N.Y. 10010
(212) 691-7753   Alan Cornet, Associate Director

Ad appearing in the May 19, 1975 issue of **The New York Times** by the American Jews Against Ford. Inset shows ad which appeared in **The Jerusalem Post** decrying Kissinger's policy of "appeasing aggressors."

Israel had fought four wars since 1948. And all they had to show for it were meaningless "pieces of paper" that each time ultimately led to yet another war.

The next step was the Geneva Conference where the Soviet leadership would have a hand in attempting a settlement. And this would be the beginning of the end!

Jewish Group Opposes Zionism

And even while these negotiations were going on, a small group of orthodox Jews based in Jerusalem, were quickly opening their own lines of communication with the Palestine Liberation Organization (PLO).

The Watchers of the City (**Neturei Karta,** in Hebrew), rather surprisingly, share the PLO's opposition to Zionism, but for quite another reason.

Their critics call them fanatics. But these Jews maintain that Israel has no right to exist until the coming of the Messiah.

This religious group believes that the Jews were sent by God into exile in punishment for sin, and until the Messiah comes, they, the Jews, should take no forcible action to regain the Holy Land.

In Yasier Arafat, leader of the PLO, they see a natural ally in their opposition to the present Jewish state.

In fact, it has been reported that if a Palestine government-in-exile would be formed, some of these anti-Zionist Jews would be included in it.

Steps to Subservience

How does the pattern of world domination change so that new governments rise to control?

We can see that pattern developing even today.

In the opinion of this author, the United States, once looked upon as the major power of the world, will soon sink into a second-rate power. The soaring debt of the United States is rapidly getting out of hand. The **debt** of the American people, of business and of government combined in 1975 was almost 3 trillion dollars! **This is nearly two thirds more than just five years ago!**

Public debt in 1975 reached the 650-billion mark.

Yet during the 1974-75 recession Americans took the attitude of "eat, drink and be merry," realizing that tomorrow offered little hope. They bought luxury-priced cars and went on a travel binge to resorts worldwide, trying to forget their problems.

Sports has become an obsession with many Americans... so much so that TV broadcasters paid $55 million last year just for the opportunity to televise football games. Now roughly 1000 hours of TV time a year are devoted to big-time sports. This is double the number in 1969.

In ancient Rome, in order to support its sports activities, they even taxed brothels. In the United States, since 1960, an estimated $1 billion worth of municipally supported arenas have been built and paid for by taxpayers. Now, with stadiums only half-filled, taxpayers will have to shell out close to $1 billion more to cover deficits.

In New Orleans, Louisiana, citizens built an enclosed Superdome. The dome itself, which was to cost $35 million and be self-supporting, now is costing some $163 million plus tens of millions in interest costs!

Contracts for players have soared to as high as $2 million for multiyear arrangements!

Meanwhile an estimated 34 million dogs in the United States require a pet-control program of some $500 million, much of it going for destroying unwanted animals.

More than $300 million was spent by Americans in 1975 to buy pets. And more than $2 billion is spent a year on pet food. The largest-selling dry or canned food item in grocery stores is pet food; four times more than baby food sales!

Besides this Americans spend about $2 billion a year on dog accessories — including gem-studded collars, perfume, gold-plated license tags, beef-flavored toothpaste and breath sprays. Dogs have their own motels, with wall-to-wall carpeting, brass beds and piped-in music.

There are stores which will outfit your dog in designer clothes. And grooming salons exist which will give your dog an egg shampoo.

Now, granted, only a few dogs enjoy such luxuries...but this is an indication of the misplaced emphasis on life that is rotting American leadership and strength and dissipating its financial stability in the eyes of the world.

Our soaring national debt, our obsession with material possessions and luxuries, our growing crime rate are but a few indicators that make it evident that soon, perhaps in the next 25 years, we will find it necessary to merge with other nations for our very existence. We are already moving in this direction and have taken the first step to subservience...a step that one day will lead to the emergence of a powerful World Leader!

In Contrast, The Hungry World

While we bask in comparative luxury, most of the world is struggling for its very life. The starving 75 million people of Bangladesh will be, according to projections, a starving 150 million people in just 25 years. The 800 million hungry people of the Indian subcontinent will balloon to 1.6 billion hungry people.

There is popular thinking today that perhaps the best approach to resolving world problems is to let people in poor nations simply starve to death. One scientist wrote in the October, 1974 issue of **BioScience:**

> Every life saved this year in a poor country diminishes the quality of life for subsequent generations.

> Every rich nation amounts to a lifeboat full of comparatively rich people. The poor of the world are in other, much more crowded lifeboats.

> Continuously, so to speak, the poor fall out of their lifeboats and swim for a little while in the water outside, hoping to be admitted to a rich lifeboat...What should the passengers on the rich lifeboat do?

> It's true we can support a great many more people than we are supporting today. If the United States turns completely vegetarian, our agriculture can support 800 million people instead of 200 million.

> But the world is increasing at 90 million people a year, so that only gives us nine years. What do you do for an encore after those nine years?

And that becomes the problem? What will happen in 1985? Will all the hopes of all the years be suddenly dampened

Too Many People Too Fast Spells Disaster in Year 2000

Billions of People

0   1   2   3   4   5   6

2000
6.1 billion
people

NOW
4 billion
people

1939
World War II
2.2 billion
people

1914
World War I
1.7 billion
people

1848
California
Gold Rush
1.1 billion
people

1776
Declaration of
Independence
850 million
people

1492
Columbus
Discovers
America
400 million
people

1215
Magna Carta
350 million
people

476
Fall of Roman
Empire
290 million
people

Birth of Christ
250 million
people

by disaster? I believe it will. Perhaps, not exactly in 1985... but by 1990!

The Club of Rome, a group of scientists and professors, seem to agree that time, indeed is running out! The very aspects of population growth are overwhelming. By the end of the next century, the world economy could be over 50 times its present size! By the year 2000, Southeast Asia will have a 30% food deficit — which will be 100% in the year 2025!

By the year 2025 world population growth **each year** will be equivalent to the total of the first 1,500 years AD!

Right now some 400 to 500 million children suffer from malnutrition worldwide. In 1965 emergency food reserves amounted to 80 days of consumption. Today, they have been reduced to under 30 days of consumption!

The Threat of Energy

Today it takes 7-8 years to construct one relatively simple nuclear reactor to provide us with power. In 100 years, with population growth quadrupled what it is today, to satisfy energy demands, we will need 3000 "nuclear parks."

Now, here's the dire consequences! Plutonium, a radioactive element, capable of self-maintained explosive fission, is used as fuel in nuclear reactors.

With proper precautions it does not present a danger. But it will become necessary, for mere human existence, to construct many more "nuclear parks" than we have today.

Scientists say it is like making a contract with the Devil in order to buy a little more time and to exist. Just ten one-millionths of a gram of Plutonium is enough to produce lung cancer. And a Plutonium ball the size of a grapefruit contains enough poison to annihilate the population of this planet!

Furthermore, plutonium's radioactivity last 25,000 years!

Clearly we have come to the end of the Golden Age.

The Center for Defense Information, a private U.S. organization, in March, 1975 stated that the United States had an arsenal of nearly 30,000 nuclear weapons, 14,800 which are stored in the U.S. and the rest scattered throughout the world. It further stated the U.S. is producing nuclear weapons at the rate of three per day.

Rear Admiral Gene R. La Rocque said:

> These weapons carry a combined explosive capability equivalent to an estimated 460 million tons of TNT — roughly 35,000 times greater than the nuclear weapon that destroyed Hiroshima in 1945.

Over 70,000 died at Hiroshima!

The Changing of Power

What does all this have to do with Israel?

Someone once said, "Nothing in the world occurs which does not, either directly or indirectly, effect everyone else."

How can the fact that the United States must dole out food stamps to some 19 million Americans effect Israel? It is but another step that one day will lead, in the author's opinion, to so taxing America's viability that it will cause America to join a European bloc of nations that will give birth to Antichrist...dreaded enemy of the Jew.

The very fact that more and more Americans are relying on government for their food and for their life...places people in a mood of subservience to a leader. The way is being prepared for tomorrow's mold of dictatorship!

And the dilemma is that in early 1975 the U.S. signed a contract worth $77 million dollars with a private American firm to teach Saudi Arabian troops how to protect the world's richest oil fields. Under this contract 1000 former U.S. servicemen are being sent to Saudi Arabia to train four battalions of the 26,000-man National Guard there.

In 1974 alone the U.S. sold over $4 billion worth of weapons to Iran, Saudi Arabia, Kuwait and Oman. This was about half the total of all foreign arms sales in 1974!

Also helping the Arab cause are the British, the French and the Soviet Union. The Soviet Union is selling tanks, fighter and attack planes, bombers and missiles to Syria and Iraq at a $2-billion-a-year pace.

In 1975 Spain bought more than $200 million worth of U.S. fighter planes. Iran purchased six fast destroyers from the U.S.

The international trade in nonnuclear arms now tops $20 billion annually — a jump of more than 550% since 1964!

And the nations of the world, in 1974 spent over $250 billion to train, equip and maintain their armed forces!

The United States (who sells freely to both Arab and Jew — and wonders why everyone doesn't love us) is easily the world's largest arms merchant...selling over $100 billion since 1950. The Soviet Union is the second largest. The U.S. shipped 600 tanks alone to Israel in 1975; and even its own army was short 1500 tanks!

Since the 1973 war, Israel has obtained more than $2 billion in supersonic fighter-bombers, tanks, bombs and ammunition.

One successful European arms trader commenting on his rising wealth said quite honestly:

We still deal in original sin.

What does this all spell? The exploding population, the rising U.S. debt, the scramble for arms superiority? Quite frankly, it spells crisis...catastrophe...and a change in the power domination of the world.

This changing of power, I believe, may occur within the next 15 years. Assassinations, coups, have a way of changing power structures overnight.

The Rise of European Supremacy

The enlarged European community has replaced the United States as the leading world trading power. Together, these European nations now have a Gross National Product that is over three-fourths that of the United States. They control three and a half times the currency reserves of the United States. In 1950, the United States held 50% of the world's monetary reserves. It now holds only 8%. But the Europe of the Nine (Common Market nations) now holds over 40%!

It has been said that great nations go through a 200-year cycle:

From bondage to freedom
From freedom back to bondage

Will this be the path the United States will take? Only time will tell.

West Germany, an economic giant, is now assuming a greater role of leadership in this time of world economic

Soviet-Israel Talks Held By Envoys in Washington

crisis. In 1974 West Germany had a $22 billion trade surplus and nearly $40 billion in gold. It was Henry Kissinger who requested that West Germany play a more active role in the Arab oil crisis, supporting the U.S. But the Europeans insist on having their own policy in the Middle East... a policy they can control!

The Day Millions Suddenly Disappear

There will come a day...no one knows when...when suddenly millions of believers will suddenly disappear from this earth! This may be hard for many readers to accept and believe.

But if they study God's Word, the Bible, they will discover that there are more than 300 Old and New Testament Scriptures which promise that Jesus Christ will come again!

And these promises will be fulfilled just as literally as the 200 Old Testament prophecies of His virgin birth, death, burial and resurrection were fulfilled in His first coming when He suffered and died for man's sin.

This event, when millions of believers disappear, is called the Rapture. It is the first phase of the events of the Second Coming of Christ.[1]

When this event occurs, the mood and character of nations may change dramatically. The alignment of nations may also change. The patterns of nation alignment and power we are witnessing today will reach their final fulfillment in the 7-year Tribulation Period which follows the Rapture.

---

[1] The Rapture refers to the time, prior to the start of the 7 year Tribulation Period, when believing Christians (both dead and alive) will "in the twinkling of an eye" be *caught up (raptured)* to meet Christ in the air. See 1 Thessalonians 4:14-17. For a comprehensive view of this event, we suggest you read GUIDE TO SURVIVAL by Salem Kirban, pp. 124-143.

The Reviving of the Roman Empire

The last of the seven Gentile world powers to persecute the nation of Israel will be the Revived Roman Empire.

What were the seven Gentile world powers? Revelation 12:3; 13:1; and 17:7 refer to these powers as seven heads. They seem to be:

1. **Egypt**
   Egypt enslaved Israel for 400 years.
   See Exodus 1-12.

2. **Assyria**
   Assyria captured and scattered the Northern Kingdom of Israel.
   See 2 Kings 17.

3. **Babylon**
   Babylon captured and took away the Southern Kingdom of Israel.
   See 2 Kings 24.

4. **Medes & Persians**
   These nations produced wicked Haman and Darius.
   See Esther 3, Isaiah 13.

5. **Greece**
   Greece brought Alexander the Great and later produced Antiochus Epiphanes, the persecutor.
   See Daniel 8 and 11.

6. **Rome**
   Rome destroyed Jerusalem in 70 AD.
   See Luke 21.

7. **Revived Roman Empire**
   The Revived Roman Empire will become Israel's greatest persecutor!
   See Revelation 12.

The old Roman Empire was quite extensive both geographically and politically. It included England, most of Europe, Asia Minor, Syria, Palestine, Egypt and the northern part of Africa.

What countries will comprise the Revived Roman Empire from which Antichrist will emerge? No one knows for certain. It would seem to cover territorially today's 9 Com-

Perhaps the greatest prize Russia wants is the vast mineral deposits in the Dead Sea.

mon Market nations which includes England. We do know, according to God's Word, that 10 nations will comprise the final bloc from which Antichrist will become leader.

I believe it is possible that the United States will become that tenth nation...going back to her mother, England, and merging with the 9 nations for her very economic existence.

There will be some who will disagree with this, of course. Only time will reveal exactly what nations will make up this revived Roman Empire structure.

How Antichrist Comes into Power

Either at sometime **prior to the Rapture** of believers or **during the first 3 1/2 years** of the 7-year Tribulation Period, Russia will take an interest in Israel's wealth.

Why would Russia want Israel?

Perhaps the great prize which Russia wants is the vast mineral deposits in the Dead Sea. The Dead Sea is 1286 feet below sea level, the lowest spot on the surface of the earth! It is 50 miles long and nine miles wide. It is still known as the "Sea of Salt" because it is filled with salt due to its having no outlet. Fed chiefly by the Jordan River, its waters have evaporated for thousands of years in the fiery heat, leaving behind an ever-growing residue of salt and other valuable minerals. It is calculated that there is enough potash in the Dead Sea to provide the needs of the entire world for 2000 years!

With a growing famine in the world, potash becomes extremely important since it is used as fertilizer. Vegetation, and consequently animal life including human life desperately require it!

But potash also has another use; that is in the making of explosives.

Russia — the Union of Soviet Socialist Republics — in area the largest country in the world — stretches across two continents from the North Pacific to the Baltic Sea. It occupies 1/6th of the earth's land surface.

So Russia, with her allies, will according to the Scriptures someday invade Israel (Ezekiel 38:1-39:16). At this time, because of Russia's march against the comparatively defenseless Jews, God's wrath is kindled:

An invalid mother visits her son's grave. Her son fell in the Yom Kippur war.

To save manpower, the high school pupils in Israel mobilized themselves for a special service into the Supply Corps where they pack combat rations.

> *And it shall come to pass at the same time when*
> *Gog [Russia] shall come against the land of Israel,*
> *saith the Lord Jehovah, that My wrath shall come*
> *up into My nostrils.*
> *(Ezekiel 38:18)*

The heavens will open and God will pour out a judgment from heaven that will wipe out the Russian military might and much of the power of the Russian confederacy.

What judgments are they?

There will be a severe earthquake and the earth around Israel will tremble severely. This earthquake will throw the soldiers into such a panic that in confusion they will kill one another.

> *...the mountains will be thrown down...every*
> *wall will fall to the ground.*
>
> *Every man's sword will be against his brother.*
> *(Ezekiel 38:20-21)*

In addition to this, sudden calamities will strike them and very violent rain and hail will fall down on them. And if this were not enough — fire and brimstone will explode right in their very midst. See Ezekiel 38:22.

Through this righteous indignation of God, we will find that the Russian armies with their allies will be destroyed without even being attacked by any other nations. All but one-sixth of the army will be killed! See Ezekiel 39:2.

What is the extent of this vast judgment?

> *Then those who inhabit the cities of Israel will*
> *go out, and make fires with the weapons and burn*
> *them, both shields and bucklers, bows and ar-*
> *rows, war clubs and spears and for seven years,*
> *they will make fires of them...For seven months*
> *the house of Israel will be burying them...Even*
> *all the people of the land will bury them.*
> *(Ezekiel 39:9,12,13)*

It takes 7 years to burn and destroy weapons and 7 months to bury the dead. So great are the casualties that it takes all of the people of Israel to help in this great task!

With this destruction of much of the Russian power, a power vacuum is created. And Antichrist rushes in to close this vacuum!

Antichrist Becomes Dictator

The ten-dictatorship confederation of nations will, for some reason, decide that one man should have rule over them. However, three of the ten nations will disagree. At this point, Antichrist, will be able to crush this rebellion, and in so doing, emerges in strength (Daniel 7:20).

A similar pattern developed during the early Hitler days, where Hitler was able, through deceitful means, to quell his opposition. Through this success he was able to become the leader not only of Germany, but also of other European nations.

Once established as the principal ruler of this 10-nation Federation, which may be called the United States of Europe, Antichrist will seek to wield his political diplomacy.

The Arab-Israeli conflict, long a sore point and threat to world peace, is, after Russia's demise in power, Antichrist's first major challenge.

The Treaty Made

Without doubt, Antichrist will present himself as a protector of Israel. In the beginning he perhaps will pledge himself to re-establish them en masse in Israel and restore to them any territory they may have ceded through treaties to the Arabs. This will probably also be a treaty of non-aggression and will be just as valid as the so-called non-

Panorama of desert shows carnage of Yom Kippur War of 1973. Israel lost over 2400 dead. This toll in a country of 3.2 million persons is comparable to the United States losing 168,000 combat dead. (The U.S. lost about 55,000 in Vietnam).

aggression treaties signed by Adolf Hitler...not worth the paper they are printed on!

It must be remembered that Israel even today does not have many friends. Its most powerful friend is the United States. But during the Arab oil embargo, when Americans were standing line for hours to buy gas...their loyalty to Israel soon diminished. Bumper stickers began to appear on cars:

FORGET ISRAEL! GIVE US ARAB OIL!

Some may forget that at one time Russia was a friend of Israel! This is evidenced by Russia's vote for the partition of Palestine, to which the Arab nations were strongly opposed, in the fall of 1947.

Now, at this point, Israel badly needs friends. And Antichrist rushes into offer her the friendship of the 10-nation federation. This treaty he makes was forseen by the prophet Daniel in Daniel 9:27,

> And he [the Antichrist; "the Prince that shall come" of verse 26] shall establish the treaty ["covenant"] with many [Israel and others] for one week [seven year period].

Undoubtedly Antichrist will be an extremely popular individual. One only has to remember Henry Kissinger as peacemaker to the Middle East to get some insight. Even though Kissinger was unable to achieve peace, and returned in defeat in March, 1975, popularity polls still showed him even more popular than the President of the United States!

With Antichrist finally being able to bring peace to the Middle East; at least a semblance of peace...his popularity will soar!

Imagine if today some great personage would rise and almost overnight resolve the Arab-Israel crisis to the satisfaction of everyone. The Arabs would go back to developing their land, and the Israeli army could at least reduce its forces to a few thousand...what a triumphal victory for the negotiator!

That's what Antichrist will be able to achieve. He will be a brilliant diplomat but also a superb strategist in the art of war.

The Egyptians have referred to Henry Kissinger as "The Magician." In 1973 alone he traveled 120,000 miles, or approximately five times around the world attempting to achieve peace.

Arriving at Lod airport, Kissinger is met by these demonstrators protesting what they believe to be a pro-Arab settlement.

His rise in power will be sudden and his popularity will be just as sudden. In today's TV age world leaders can be given immediate popularity overnight. Within a few seconds of its occurring, their exploits of victory are transmitted worldwide via the video screen!

The world will become very enthusiastic about his reign. Indeed some marvelous things may be produced at that time. Great new cities may be built and science may make some startling discoveries.

If you live during the reign of Antichrist...don't be fooled by his message of peace...for his main purpose is to bring a reign of death and destruction.

This will be an era of false security. It will last just 3½ years...the first 3½ years of the 7-year Tribulation Period.

The Treaty Broken

By the middle of the Tribulation Period, Israel will have fully served Antichrist's usefulness. He wielded Israel friendship only to serve his own ends...those ends were to make him a world leader. Now, that Antichrist is looked upon as the world leader, all-powerful, he no longer needs the so-called alliance with Israel.

And he is antagonized by Israel's growing glory and independence.

So, this man, who at his merest whim, can change the course of nations, will break his treaty with Israel and order their ceremonial worship to their Lord to cease. No longer may they make sacrifices to their God...their full allegiance must be to Antichrist who they should regard along with the rest of the world as the Saviour!

It is this step that ushers in the day Israel dies!

3 DECISIVE WARS

War	Participants	Occurs	Reason for War	Outcome	Scripture References
1	Russia and Allies (Arab nations, Iran, Germany) vs. Israel	Before or during first 3½ years of Tribulation Period (This could happen at any time!)	Russia desires Israel's vast mineral wealth.	God will intervene and through an earthquake in Israel plus rain and hail, the Russian army will be wiped out. It will take the Israelites 7 years to collect the debris. It will also take them 7 months to bury the dead!	Ezekiel 38:1–39:16
2 Battle of Armageddon	Armies from All Nations vs. God at Jerusalem	At End of 7 year Tribulation Period	Flushed with power Antichrist will defy God, seek to destroy the 144,000 witnessing Jews and Jerusalem.	The Lord Jesus Christ comes down from heaven and wipes out the combined armies of more than 200 million men. The blood bath covers over 185 miles of Israel and is "even unto the horse bridles." (Revelation 14:20) Antichrist and the False Prophet are cast alive into the Lake of Fire. (Revelation 19:20) Satan is bound in the bottomless pit for 1000 years. (Revelation 20:1-3)	Joel 3:9, 12 Zechariah 14:1-4 Revelation 16:13-16 Revelation 19:11-21 Ezekiel 39:17-29
3 The Final Rebellion	Satan vs. God	At End of 1000 year Millennium Period	God allows Satan one more opportunity on earth to preach his deceiving message.	Satan will be successful in deceiving vast multitudes (out of those born during the millennial period) to turn away from Christ. This horde of perhaps millions of people will completely circle the Believers in Jerusalem in a state of siege. When this occurs, God brings FIRE down from Heaven killing the millions in Satan's army. Satan is then cast into the Lake of Fire, where the False Prophet and Antichrist are, and they will be tormented day and night for ever and ever.	Revelation 20:7-10

Israel flag in a lookout on Kuneitra, the ghost town in the
Golan Heights, which was returned to the Syrians.

A resident of Mettula — Israel's northernmost village —
on the Lebanese border, turns up for target practice.

Young women lay barb wire at Israel's border.

Tel Aviv defense workers practice installing and using an emergency water system to prepare for an eventual war.

Israeli women soldiers check their automatic weapons. Women serve in the armed forces for 2 years; men, 3 years.

Symbolizing the plight of Syrian Jewery, students demon-
strate in Tel Aviv.

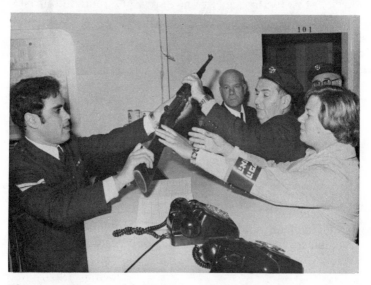

The Israeli Government uses Civil Defense to prevent
terrorist activity. Unit includes many women volunteers
who carry rifles.

12

THE DAY ISRAEL DIES!

Now that the apostate church has furthered the ambitions of Antichrist, with Israel also being deceived by him, Antichrist has no further use for the nation of Israel. Antichrist's power base is now strong enough that he no longer needs to pretend a love for that nation.

The time: the middle of the Tribulation Period.

Russia is no more the major power, having had many of her armies destroyed in her attempt to invade Israel (Ezekiel 38:1 — 39:16).

Antichrist did not learn a lesson from this act of God. In fact, Antichrist may actually—for a time—believe that he is acting in God's interest.

You will recall when the Assyrian king, Sennacherib, attempted to invade Jerusalem, his general said to the Jewish people:

> Have I now come up without the Lord's approval
> against this place to destroy it? The Lord said to
> me, "Go up against this land and destroy it..."
> *(2 Kings 18:25)*

Adolf Hitler, who was responsible for the death of millions of Jews, also invoked the blessing of God when he said:

> We are all proud that through God's powerful aid
> we have once more become true Germans.

In fact, even today there are many malicious world leaders

who use God's name as license for wholesale murder and tyranny.

When one has power, one wants more power. To many an unregenerate mind, there is little else to strive for.

It was the Roman historian Tacitus who said way back in the First Century AD that

> *The lust for power, for dominating others, inflames the heart more than any other passion.*

And Lord Acton, in a letter in 1887, observed:

> *Power tends to corrupt; absolute power corrupts absolutely.*

And Antichrist comes to the point in his reign where he does achieve absolute power and such power will bring a reign of terror on Jew and Gentile alike.

The Day Temple Sacrifices Cease

One might ask, who is this Antichrist? Where does he come from? There is much speculation on this subject.

In Daniel 9:27 we read:

> *And he [Antichrist] will make a firm covenant with many for one week [The 7-year Tribulation Period], but in the middle of the week [after 3½ years] he will put a stop to sacrifice and grain offering*

Let's pause here just for a moment to recall for you that this is not the first time that the people of Israel are stopped from making their sacrifices at the Temple.

This occurred during the oppressions of Nebuchadnezzar, Antiochus IV Epiphanes, Pompey, and Titus.

> *And on the wing of abominations will come one who makes desolate, even until a complete destruction, one that is decreed, is poured out on the one who makes desolate.*
> > *(Daniel 9:27 continued)*

What this is saying is that Antichrist who will bring the greatest sorrow to the Jew, will in the end be completely defeated by God.

But where does he come from?

Perhaps Daniel 9:26 give us some hint as to his origin:

> After the 62 weeks the Messiah will be cut off
> and have nothing...
> and the people of the prince who is to come will
> destroy the city [Jerusalem] and the sanctuary.

Who are the "people of the prince"?

The people of the prince is the old Roman empire. Therefore Antichrist most likely will emerge from a nation that was in this old Roman empire. Of course, the empire at that time included many nations for Rome ruled the world.

The old Roman empire included what is now Great Britain, Germany, much of Europe, the Palestinian Arab countries, Egypt and North Africa, and what is now Israel.

You can see that this leaves many areas from which Antichrist could emerge. In fact, in my opinion, Antichrist could emerge from the United States, since the United States through its mother, Great Britain, could be considered as coming out of the great Roman empire.

The fortunes of nations change almost overnight. New world leaders spring up just as suddenly as old ones die off or are assassinated.

On Tuesday, March 25, 1975, King Faisal of Saudi Arabia, America's staunch friend in the Arab world, was assassinated by his nephew.

One American official, upon being notified of Faisal's death said:

> *My God, it couldn't come at a worse time!*

Why?

Because Henry Kissinger, after 17 days of continuous commuting, had just returned back to the United States stating that his efforts of negotiating between Egypt and Israel had ended in failure.

No one knows what tomorrow will bring...what world leader, now an unknown, will suddenly emerge on the scene.

We do know that in recent years we have seen new powerful leaders take over countries that were once thought to be very stable and secure.

The death of King Faisal left a temporary power vacuum.

The first trees of the 150,000 tree forest planned for the new town of Yamit are planted by several hundred teachers from Tel Aviv.

Time for a break from military manuevers in the desert.

Daniel Foresaw Israel's Persecution

In Daniel 9:24 God revealed through Daniel the following:

> *The Lord has commanded 490 years of further struggle upon Jerusalem and your people.*

This is commonly referred to as the Seventy Weeks of Daniel. The phrase "seventy weeks" literally means **70 sevens** or 490 years.

Here is how they break down:

The first division: 7 sevens (49 years)

This covers the 49 years for the rebuilding of Jerusalem. See Nehemiah and Ezra 1:1-4. This decree may have been one issued in 453 BC by Cyrus or the one in 445 BC by Axtaxerxes, the Persian King.

The second division: 62 sevens (434 years)

From the completion of the city of Jerusalem (at the end of the 49 years as described in Nehemiah) to the time Jesus Christ is crucified (cut off)

The third division: 1 seven (7 years)

This covers the Tribulation Period

Now what God tells us in His Word through Daniel is:

> *...you are to know and discern that from the issuing of a decree to restore and rebuild Jerusalem [Nehemiah 2:1-8] until Messiah the Prince there will be 49 years and 434 years...*
>
> *(Daniel 9:25)*

This has already occurred. Christ was crucified some 2000 years ago.

Now, during this era since His crucifixion, is a pause in time.

The clock of prophecy is at a standstill. It will start running again to begin the last 7 years of terror after the Rapture occurs.

This is the seven years of Tribulation as revealed in Daniel 9:26-27.

Antichrist...A Personality of Power

What type of character would produce an Antichrist? Daniel gives us some insight as to the personality of this man.

> And in the latter period of their rule, When the transgressors have run their course, A king will arise Insolent and skilled in intrigue
> (Daniel 8:23)[1]

Antichrist will be an intellectual genius one whose true character will show a bold rudeness and insensitivity to the feelings of others.

> His power will be mighty, but not by his own power, And he will destroy to an extraordinary degree And prosper and perform his will; He will destroy mighty men and the holy people.
> (Daniel 8:24)

This reveals that the power of Antichrist will come from Satan himself. Satan gives him as much power as he possibly can and with this power Antichrist will be known as a destroyer of men.

His blitzkrieg tactics will make him prosperous and for a time nothing will stand in his way. People will simply accept his edicts. This blitzkrieg technique is not new. It has been practiced by many tyrants; the most recent, perhaps, being Adolf Hitler, who almost singlehandedly took control of Germany.

His power will be so great that for a time he will be able to destroy even Israel.

We are further told:

> And through his shrewdness He will cause deceit to succeed by his influence; And he will magnify himself in his heart, And he will destroy many while they are at ease.
> (Daniel 8:25)

---

[1]Daniel 8:23-25 takes us to the "latter period," which is either to the time of Antichrist, or to the time of Antiochus IV Epiphanes who is the "type" of Antichrist—his prophetic portrait.

Antichrist...Master of Deception

Antichrist will be the master of deception! He will be able to defeat many by catching them off guard as they bask in false security.

Here is a leader, who for the first 3½ years, has brought about a relative peace, has become very popular. Now, while everyone is relaxing, suddenly his blitzkrieg tactics are employed and without prior warning, he comes in for the power kill.

So assured of his power will he be that he will even take on God.

Most great leaders have a tremendous charisma, that special quality that gives an individual influence or authority over large numbers of people. No doubt Antichrist will possess this atribute. He will also be a great orator. Just as Hitler persuasive speeches could hold and move crowds, so Antichrist will possess such power. Hitler's theory was the bigger the lie, the easier for people to believe. How coincidental with what Daniel had prophesied about Antichrist:

> The king [Antichrist] will do as he pleases, and he will exalt and magnify himself above every god, and will speak monstrous things against the God of gods...
>
> *(Daniel 11:36)*

Antichrist will also be a political genius. In Revelation 17:11-12 we are told that Antichrist will be able to merge together 10 nations and become their ruler.

Antichrist will be able to control human life:

> And he causes all, the small and the great, and the rich and the poor, and the free men and the slaves, to be given a mark on their right hand, or on their forehead,
>
> And he provides that no one should be able to buy or to sell, except the one who has the mark, either the name of the beast or the number of his name.
>
> *(Revelation 13:16-17)*

He will be considered a great general, a military genius. He will win battles and will come back to his home base as a conquering hero.

Many, realizing his military strength will exclaim:

> Where is there anyone as great as he? Who is able to fight against him?
>
> (Revelation 13:4)

He will be looked on as a religious leader by many. So great will be his exploits that he will be worshiped as a god.

> And all who dwell on the earth will worship him, every one whose name has not been written from the foundation of the world in the book of life of the Lamb [Jesus Christ] who has been slain.
>
> (Revelation 13:8)

No man in history will have all these attributes in such great power as with Antichrist!

The Master Plan Begins

It seems ironic that Theodor Herzl, the father of political Zionism, should write in his diary on October 31, 1898:

> When I remember thee in days to come, O Jerusalem, it will not be with delight.
>
> The musty deposits of two thousand years of inhumanity, intolerance, and foulness lie in your reeking alleys. The one man who has been present here all this while, the lovable dreamer of Nazareth, has done nothing but help increase the hate.[1]

One can understand what made Herzl make this statement for starting with the Egyptians, under Pharoah, the Assyrians, the Babylonians, the Medes and Persians, the Greeks, the Romans...the age of the Gentiles...the Jewish people have known nothing but oppression. And because in the Middle Ages and after, this persecution of the Jew often came from the hands of men wearing large crosses, we can understand Herzl's error in equating Christ and Christianity with these oppressors.

The Temple, Sacred to Jewish History

Before we go further we should realize that to the Jew, the Temple holds the most sacred place in his heart. Knowing

---

[1] *The Diaries of Theodor Herzl*, New York: Dial Press, 1956, p. 283.

this, many tyrants of the past have sought to desecrate the Jewish Temple; Antiochus IV being among the most noted. It was Antiochus IV who placed a swine on the altar for sacrifice...the height of sacrilege since God, under the Mosaic law, pronounced the swine as unclean.

Because the Temple is the focal point for Antichrist's horrible actions, let us see how the Temple progressed in Jewish history.

The inspiration for the first Temple plan came to David. He delivered to Solomon the "pattern" for the Temple (1 Chronicles 28:11) that he had received by God's Spirit (28:12) and in writing (28:19).

No expense was spared in building this Temple. David, in fact, gave all his own private treasures to aid in the construction, in addition to the building materials he had already collected (1 Chronicles 29:3).

His personal contribution consisted of:

1. $85,000,000 worth of gold from Ophir;
2. $20,000,000 worth of purest silver for overlaying the walls.

And besides these the heads of the tribes of Israel, the army officers and the administrative officers of David pledged:

1. $145,000,000 in gold;
2. $30,000,000 in silver;
3. 800 tons of bronze;
4. 4600 tons of iron.

For a modern day comparison of such generosity one only has to look at the millions of dollars concerned Jews contribute today so that Israel may have adequate defenses.

Remember, these large amounts of money expended on the Temple were made in the days before 20th Century inflation. This should give you some idea as to the splendour of Solomon's Temple.

And it took about 200,000 workmen 7 years and 6 months to build this Temple!

Why would the Jews build a Temple in the first place?

Because God commanded them to. And because the Temple

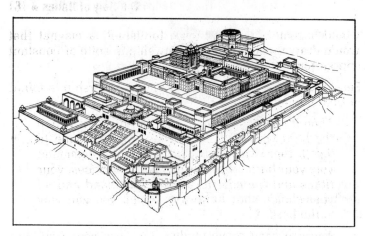

The First Temple, built during Solomon's reign over a period of seven years, was destroyed by Nebuchadnezzar, king of Babylon in 586 BC.

The Second Temple was erected about 70 years later, then rebuilt in the 1st century with unusual splendor by Herod. This Temple was destroyed by the soldiers of Titus in 70 AD. Today the Dome of the Rock occupies the site of the Temple.

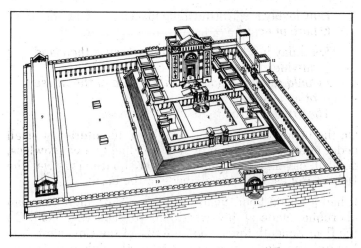

would become a unifying force for Israel...a magnet that would draw them into close fellowship in spite of constant oppression.

Perhaps the first command for a place of worship is found in Deuteronomy 12:11-12:

> Then it shall come about that the place in which the Lord your God shall choose for His name to dwell, there you shall bring all that I command you: your burnt offerings and your sacrifices, your tithes and the contribution of your hand and all your choice votive offerings which you will vow to the Lord.

> And you shall rejoice before the Lord your God, you and your sons and daughters, your male and female servants...

The sanctity of the Temple was unique in that, once it was built, only from there could sacrifices be offered in obedience to the Law.

Psalm 84 is the Psalm of one longing to worship in the Temple. In part it says:

> How lovely are Thy dwelling places,
> O Lord of hosts!

> For a day in Thy courts is better than a thousand
>   outside.
> I would rather stand at the threshold of the house
>   of my God,
> Than dwell in the tents of wickedness.

On the inside of Solomon's Temple, in its interior, a small cedar altar stood in front of steps leading to a windowless, cubical, cavelike room about 30 feet square. This was the Holy of Holies, the special abode of the Lord.

It had a raised floor. Inside were two 15-ft.-high guardian cherubim, made of olivewood and adorned with gold. On the floor beneath them stood the Ark of the Covenant. The Holy of the Holies was entered by the high priest only, and this on but one day in the year, the day of atonement!

It would take a world leader of great insolence and arrogance to enter such a holy place and desecrate it!

Today the nation of Israel is barred from building their Temple because the Dome of the Rock is on the site which is so revered by the Jews. One day through a war or an earthquake, the Dome of the Rock will be destroyed. Outlined in the photo is the Wailing Wall. This is a portion of the western wall of Herod's Temple preserved by the Romans when they destroyed the city in 70 A.D. to show how formidable they were.

The Three Temples

Solomon's Temple was the first of Three Temples. All these stood in succession upon the same site on Mount Moriah in Jerusalem. The other two Temples were Zerubbabel's Temple and Herod's Temple.[1]

Solomon's Temple, built in 970 BC was destroyed in 586 BC by the Babylonians, under Nebuchadnezzar.

The Temple known as the Second Temple was built under Zerubbabel, the ruler of the exiled Jews who had returned from Babylon to Jerusalem. This Temple was begun in 534 BC and lasted more than 100 years longer than Solomon's Temple.

The Second Temple became dilapidated.

It was in about 20 B.C. that Herod the Great undertook the restoration of the Temple. The work was not completed until 64 AD. This was known as Herod's Temple. But in 70 AD the Temple was destroyed by fire in the siege of Jerusalem by the army of Titus.

Today the Temple site is now occupied partially by the Dome of the Rock. A portion of a western wall which stood outside of Herod's temple was preserved by the Romans when they destroyed the city to show how formidable they were. This fragment of wall is revered by the Jews and called The Wailing Wall.

In a period of a little over 1000 years the Jews had a Temple. But now, for over 1900 years they have been without a Temple.

One can imagine the rapturous joy the Jew will experience when finally, in Jerusalem, they build their Temple again. With the wealth of Solomon's Temple, it is hard to vision how costly, how jewelled-appointed will be this next Temple. It will probably excel in cost and in beauty almost every existing current structure in the world.

It will be a project that will serve as perhaps the most moving unifying force the Jews have ever had since the days of Solomon. So revered will it be, that Jews will lay

---

[1] It is customary, however, in Israel to speak of only two temples. Solomon's, of course, was the First. Then, since the Temple built by Herod in 16-18 B.C. only refaced and put new siding on the earlier Second Temple of Zerubbabel, it is still considered to be only part of this same Second Temple.

down their lives rather than allow its holiness to be compromised.

And, yet, it will be to this Temple that Antichrist, through Satan, will impose his most disgraceful act, known in Scriptures as the abomination of desolation.

The Abomination of Desolation

The Abomination will be some awful, detestable thing that leaves the entire Temple desolate, dirty and empty. Not since Antiochus IV slaughtered pigs on the alter in the Holy of Holies and placed the idol of Jupiter in the Temple has Israel witnessed a blasphemy.

Yet this future action is part of Antichrist's master plan to break Israel's will and conquer and subdue the nation.

Antichrist is a man of whom Scriptures say, his "...power will be great, but not by his own power" (Daniel 8:24).

What does this mean..."not by his own power"?

Antichrist will be able through his armies to supress Russia, and to crush the Arab countries. His power will be worldwide. But where does he get this power? Revelation 13:2 gives us the answer:

Israeli soldiers say their early morning prayers at front.

> *...the dragon [Satan] gave him [Antichrist] his power and his throne and great authority.*

Now there have been many world leaders who we perhaps thought were Satan-inspired because of their actions. But, in this world leader, Antichrist, Satan will give all the power he possibly can.

Actually this world leader will be part of the Satanic trinity. Just as there is a Heavenly Trinity (Father, Son and Holy Spirit), the Bible reveals there is also a Satanic trinity (Satan, the Antichrist, and the False Prophet).

The Bible sometimes refers to Antichrist as The Beast because he becomes the leader of the endtime Beast empire (Revelation 13; Daniel 7). But he will be a human being inspired by Satan.

> **Satan** imitates the work of **God the Father.**
> **The Beast (Antichrist)** imitates the work of the **Son** in subjecting the world to himself.
> **The False Prophet** imitates the work of the **Holy Spirit** in praising the false king (Antichrist) who will reign on this world's throne.

This great world leader, Antichrist, while coming to power at the beginning of the 7-year Tribulation period, will show his true character of tyranny in the last 3½ years of this period.

A Pseudo-Religious Leader Aids Antichrist

Assisting him in his diabolical scheme will be a pseudo-religious leader. In the Scriptures he is called The False Prophet.

We also find during the tribulation period that ten world leaders will have surrendered their power to one man, Antichrist. Antichrist, in order to let a type of religious system prevail temporarily, appoints an associate, an imitation religious leader, to carry out his instructions. Perhaps the reasoning behind this is that Antichrist, who is known for his cunning tactics, wishes to use the church movement to achieve his own sinister goals. The actions that follow seem to confirm this.

Where does this False Prophet reside?

It would appear from reading Revelation 17:9 that his residence would be in Rome. Verse 9 indicates that this religious system has its residence in a city built on seven hills or mountains.

This False Prophet will be able to perform unexplainable miracles. While everyone watches he will be able to make fire flame down to earth from the skies. See Revelation 13:13.

We also know he will come with a lamb-like appearance, but when he speaks it will be with the authority and actions of Satan (Revelation 13:12).

So great will be his power and his miracles that people will follow him and accept everything he says as gospel truth.

So, in the False Prophet, Antichrist, the world leader has a powerful ally to help him achieve his ends.

Brings a Dead Man Back to Life

The False Prophet will be a miracle worker. In fact, his greatest miracle is described in Revelation 13:14 when he somehow causes a statue to come to life and speak.

As we try to construct from the Scriptures what may occur, it would appear that during the first 3½ years of the Tribulation period, Antichrist will be somehow killed (Revelation 13:3). But then he will reappear alive (Revelation 13:3,12)! The False Prophet will make an image or a statue of this Antichrist probably in the city of Jerusalem.

He will have the power somehow to make this image come to life and to speak and demand that all who will not worship it be put to death. Here is where the Mark is applied to the hand or forehead (Revelation 13:14-18).

What actually will occur when Antichrist receives "...the wound of the sword..." cannot be ascertained as detailed as we would like. We must await their fulfillment in time to completely understand what occurs.

But we can see how that when this event does take place, it will have such impact that the entire world will worship Antichrist. And this is not difficult to understand. Lenin, considered the father of Communism is still visible today in a glass-topped tomb in Moscow. And daily, thousands stand in line to view him. And although he is a native of

Russia, he is revered by staunch communists worldwide including China, parts of South America, Africa and in parts of Arab nations. In the early 1900's even some naive Jews joined the multitude which hailed Lenin as their hope for deliverance from oppression. Imagine the thinking of millions of people if suddenly the Archbishop of the Russian Orthodox Church in Russia could somehow bring Lenin back to life. The whole world would gasp in amazement and Lenin would be hailed as God.

The Terror Begins

The False Prophet, in order to transfer even greater allegiance and power to his leader, Antichrist, takes what he believes is his most brilliant step as he:

> ...causes all, the small and the great, and the rich and the poor, and the free man and the slave, to be given a mark on their right hand, or on their forehead.
>
> (Revelation 13:16)

The False Prophet in his edict does not let anyone get away with not accepting the Mark to show his allegiance to the great Leader, the Antichrist. And his reason for this marking system is so that:

> no one should be able to buy or to sell, except the one who has the mark, either the name of the beast [Antichrist] or the number of his name... and his number is six hundred and sixty-six.
>
> (Revelation 13:17-18)

Now this identification system is not new. During the Middle Ages Jews were marked by a Papal-backed Spain which forced the Jews to wear a yellow identification badge. Similar decrees, sponsored always by "the Church," were enforced in England in 1218, in France in 1219 and in Hungary in 1279.

And most will remember Hitler's serial number marking which was tattooed on millions of Jews in concentration camps.

Even Protestants came under a marking system during the religious quarrels in France in the 1500's and 1600's. The

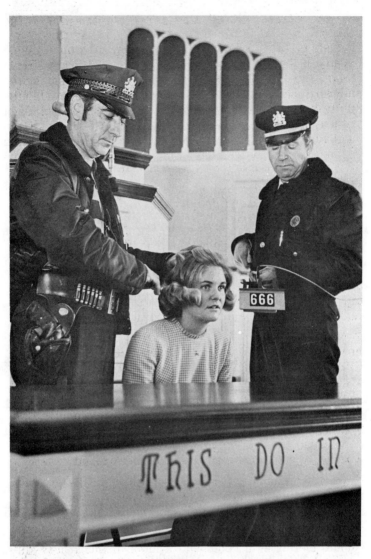

Some marking system will identify those loyal to Antichrist. The Mark will be placed either on the right hand or on the forehead. See Revelation 13:16.

Huguenots, who followed the teachings of John Calvin, became a large political group in France. As they grew strong, the Catholic government persecuted them more and more. The time came when they were no longer able to buy or sell; almost all offices and trades were forbidden to them and in the Massacre of Saint Bartholomew's Day on August 24, 1572, thousands of Huguenots were murdered.

Today's Marking System, Tomorrow's Control

One might ask the question, how could intelligent people allow themselves to be deluded into accepting a Mark so they could buy or sell.

The answer is simple. We are **already** accepting systems of identification control. The Social Security number, initiated in the 1930's, as a means only of identifying an individual to see that he received his payments, has almost become a universal identification number in the United States. It is requested when you apply for a job, when you apply for a loan, when you apply for a license plate, etc.

In 1975 the U.S. Passport office suggested everyone in the U.S. be given a unified identification number. The advent of credit cards has also advanced the numbering idea. Soon cash will be outdated. Even checks will be phased out of existence in a few years. All or most transactions will be through a plastic credit card that has a number. That number, when passed through a computer, will determine whether or not you can buy merchandise or food.

Now, what food companies have hailed as the greatest invention since the light bulb, has been the creation of a series of vertical stripes on all supermarket items.

This new Universal Product Code is known to most consumers merely as a composite symbol of black bars and numbers appearing on many packages.

When drawn across a scanner at the supermarket checkout station, the symbol identifies the item to a computer, which instantaneously tells the cash register what price to ring up for that product. Within 10 years every supermarket in the United States will have this computer system in operation, controlling the identification of over 200 billion cans, packages and bottles, annually!

But that's not all. An Ohio company, in early 1975, was

issued a patent that has an identification apparatus which relies on the characteristic vibrations of the human body.

Acoustical [sound] wave energy can be transmitted from one finger to another and be recorded for later reference!

As an example, this procedure can identify a person who stands on a doormat and places one hand on a doorknob. If the frequency response passing through the body matches the one recorded in the memory device, the applicant is admitted. The characteristics of several thousand individuals can be stored in **one** memory device!

The inventor says this system will be used to provide access to computers and verify credit cards and bank checks.

Special credit cards have also been designed that are used instead of keys to unlock doors!

What does this all mean? And how does it affect the Jew? One must keep in mind that in this last 3½ year Tribulation Period not only Jews, but also all Gentiles who turn to Christ (the tribulation saints) will be persecuted.

And these sophisticated computer systems, which are already in use...to select those eligible to buy food, to be admitted into a house...will be used to identify those with the approved Mark!

It is conceivable that the population explosion will be so acute that housing facilities, as well as food, will be in short supply. Naturally those who are loyal to Antichrist, who wear his emblem or Mark, will be those thought worthy to buy food and seek housing.

Without the Mark, it may be impossible for you to enter your own home! Your finger vibrations may not be in the memory bank of the lock on your house nor in that of the supermarket where you shop.

Now can you see how events of today make it entirely possible for Antichrist's action of tomorrow?

The Enforcer

How will the False Prophet enforce his edict? One can imagine the pandemonium that breaks out when this announcement is first made to the public. People will rush to the grocery stores to stock up on food perhaps only to find the stores bolted shut until the marking system has been completed.

In November, 1974 when I was in Israel, the Israeli pound was devalued some 60%. People panicked. They flocked into appliance stores trying to buy refrigerators. They crowded into their grocery stores hoarding up on food. When the appliance dealer told them he was sold out of refrigerators they asked: "What else do you have, I'll buy anything!" Such was the mass hysteria of the first few days. Some stores closed, hiding their goods, knowing that with the raise in prices they would soon realize a bigger profit.

Naturally, the False Prophet will need a company of loyal soldiers to enforce his edict. And no doubt, he will have a spy system that would make the Gestapo, the Russian K.G.B. and the United States C.I.A. turn green with envy.

Such an effective spy system would be necessary for the enforcement of a loyal world government.

In an expanded edition of his book **American Foreign Policy** published by Norton in 1974, Henry Kissinger states:

> We must construct an international order before a crisis imposes it as a necessity.

In a speech given in Los Angeles on January 24, 1975 he said that the last quarter of this century

> could be remembered as that period when mankind fashioned the first truly global community.

Dr. Kissinger further stated:

> There can be no peaceful international order without a constructive relationship between the United States and the Soviet Union...

Would such a constructive relationship include the working together of the K.G.B. and the C.I.A.? In light of Bible prophecy, this could be a future possibility.

It was Felix Dzerzhinksy, Russia's first secret police chief, who said:

> We stand for organized terror.

Nor is the C.I.A. above approach, or the leaders of Government. The C.I.A. has admitted that at times it has operated outside of the scope of their authorization, illegally. And the Watergate scandal during the Nixon administration should certainly make people aware of the intrigue, the lies and the power struggle that attempted to thwart the freedom of Americans.

Alexander Solzhenitsyn in his book, **The Gulag Archipelago** (New York, Harper and Row, 1973) told how the K.G.B. extract "confessions." Beginning with night arrests, they employ every manner of humiliation to break their victims, including thirst, filth, drugs, deprivation of sleep, threatening loved ones, insect-infested boxes, starvation, the gradual crushing of genitals, scraping the skin off a man's back with a grater till it bled and then oiling it with turpentine!

The Choice: To Bow or to Starve

Imagine if you were living in the Tribulation Period. You had a choice: to accept the Mark and be able to buy food and life...or to reject the Mark and face persecution and hunger. Slowly you watch as your baby cries in anguish

Imagine the anguish if you went with your grocery bag to the supermarket and found you could not buy food because you did not have the approved identification mark!

from starvation. Perhaps you witness your husband torn away from you. Held down by soldiers, he is injected with heroin day after day until he is totally relying on the drug. Then, a walking automaton, he is released back to you! How long could you stand it? Would you finally break and accept the Mark? Or would it take some more coaxing like watching your 5-year-old child slowly die by starvation? Would this be the breaking point?

How strong would be your faith? That is just the beginning of what both Jew and Christ-believing Gentile Tribulation Saint may face in the torturous last 3½ years of the Tribulation Period.

When something like this is brought to our attention, we tend to disbelieve it, saying that it will never occur. Yet we fail to realize that such brutality is occurring even today!

Even the world-famous Canadian royal Mounted Police, as recently as 1975, have used a 39-page manual of instruction as their basis for breaking down an individual. The manual advocates the use of brainwashing, sexism, lies, deceit and deprivation as an "assault on his dignity."[1]

Imagine the day when you cannot automatically go to the supermarket to buy food...when your freedoms will be so restricted that you and your loved ones may die of starvation, and most won't care.

But, of course, this is not new either. Right now throughout the world thousands of children die of starvation every day but even you and I are indifferent to the plight. Why? Perhaps, because we are so busy just trying to keep ourselves alive! And this indifference will be amplified during the Tribulation Period.

Imagine the scoffs of the crowd:

> So they're starving...it's their own fault. If they would accept the Mark, they would live and have the food they need. Instead, it's their choice for them to follow their God. See if their God will send them manna from Heaven. If he did it once... let him do it again!

Loaded with their bag of groceries, the people will not pity those who refuse to accept the Mark.

---

[1] *Philadelphia Inquirer*, UPI, Philadelphia: March 27, 1975, p. 3-A.

Israel's Greatest Humiliation

Up till the middle of the 7-year Tribulation Period, Antichrist will have manuevered the nation of Israel into a position that gives him greater world power. His ability to temporarily resolve the Arab-Israeli conflict makes him a hero. Naturally, for a few years, he must show evidences of kindness towards Israel.

But, deep within his heart, there is a burning resentment. He fears Israel will become too strong, too independent and not subservient to him. He watches as Israel builds her Temple. He notices how this Temple...the first for over 2000 years...has a unifying effect upon the Jew. He sees them bring their treasures of wealth to the Temple. He sees rich and poor alike enter with tears streaming down their face. And this disturbs him greatly.

Somehow, something must be done to crush Israel so he, Antichrist, can have world domination. How often the so-called Saviours of the world show their true colors and become oppressors! And Antichrist appeared at first to have become the chief deliverer of Israel. Now is the time to make his move!

In Daniel 9:27 we are told:

> ...he [Antichrist] shall make a firm covenant with many for one week [7 years]; and in the midst of the week [3½ years] he shall cause sacrifice and offering to cease....

It is at this midpoint of the 7 years that Antichrist, flushed with power, will move in on Israel to stop the religious ceremonies of the Jews in the Temple. This will be Israel's greatest humiliation.

The Mark and the Seal

Prior to this occurring some Jews will receive a protective seal from God. This is in contrast to the Mark imposed by Antichrist in order to buy or to sell. In the case of the Mark, those who refuse to accept it, both Jew and Gentile alike, will suffer and many will die.

But between the breaking of the Sixth Seal and the Seventh Seal judgments, right after vast earthquakes occur and meteors fall to earth...we see an interval of time.

This will be a time in which 144,000 of the children of Israel, 12,000 from each of the 12 tribes, will be "sealed."

While the Mark of Antichrist will be either on the hand or forehead, God will place this seal of protection on their foreheads (Revelation 7:3).

> And I saw another angel ascending from the rising of the sun, having the seal of the living God; and he cried out with a loud voice to the four angels to whom it was granted to harm the earth and the sea, saying, "Do not harm the earth or the sea or the trees, until we have sealed the bond-servants of our God on their foreheads."
>
> And I heard the number of those who were sealed, one hundred and forty-four thousand sealed from every tribe of the sons of Israel.
>
> (Revelation 7:2-4)

This seal, as described in the verse just quoted, will be the mark of God and will identify them as God's chosen witnesses during the Tribulation Period. And the amazing thing is that neither Antichrist nor the False Prophet nor Satan will be able to stop them from witnessing to their faith in Christ.

There will not be one Gentile in these 144,000! **They will all be Jews.** As to their actual identity, as far as the present is concerned, no one knows who they will be. But God will know who they are even though they may now be scattered among the nations.

It is quite conceivable that they will witness to the millions of Jews in the Holy Land and throughout the world just prior to the exodus of the Jews from Jerusalem. Let's take a moment to set the scene.

Just prior to God placing His seal on the 144,000, the Fourth Seal of judgment has just been released. This is a judgment of death which includes war, famine and disease. We are told in Revelation 6:7-8 that as a result of this judgment one-fourth of the population of the land will be destroyed!

> If the word "land" (or "earth") refers to the entire globe, and if we went on the basis of our present population...this would mean that some 800 million people or more will die through various judgments at this time! It may, however, only refer to Eur-asia or to Palestine. In any case there will be mass death.

THE NEW YORK TIMES, FRIDAY, MAY 1, 1970

Christianity Linked to Pollution

By EDWARD B. FISKE
Special to The New York Times

CLAREMONT, Calif., April 30 —A group of Protestant theologians asserted here today that Christianity had played its part in provoking the current environ~~~~ ~~~~ ~~~~ and

Scholars Cite Call in Bible for Man to Dominate Life

major paper of the conference~~~~

be the object of the same love that is directed to human beings.

The theologian said that because it was impossible for people to "believe something simply because it seem~~~~

Right after this catastrophe, undoubtedly many will blame these judgments on the Christians. And this is not new. During the ecology campaigns of the late 1960's and early 1970's several ecological writers blamed the ills of the world on the verse in Genesis 1:28 which says:

> ...and God said to them, "Be fruitful and multiply, and fill the earth, and subdue it...

And, in effect, they said that Christians were to blame for the world conditions of today. They argued that Bible believers were only concerned with "subduing" the earth, and that they did not have any concern with preserving the earth.

Such accusations, during this Tribulation Period will, of course, be magnified particularly in light of the fact that believers will refuse to accept the Mark of Antichrist.

As a result, in the breaking of the Fifth Seal judgment we find many, many believers martyred (Revelation 6:9-11). Such martyrdom may well come in the form of beheading. And seeing, how in the future Antichrist will desecrate the Temple of the Jews, it would not be surprising if such mass beheadings took place right on Church lawns in front of thousands of spectators, as an example to others! See Revelation 20:4 which reveals that many believers, because of their testimony, will be beheaded!

We are telling you all this to give you the background of what has just occurred.

For it is right after this terrible persecution of the believers that God seals the 144,000 Jews to protect them from this horrible fate and so they might be able to witness of their Messiah to the remaining faithful gentiles who have turned to Christ and to the still non-believing Jews.

What exactly will these 144,000 preach?

They will preach the same Gospel that Paul and Peter preached; that men are in need of a Saviour; that Jesus Christ died for the remission of sins to provide eternal life for all who but believe!

These 144,000 will not be stationed solely in Jerusalem, but will very possibly be in every part of the globe. And apparently they will all be as effective as a Dwight L. Moody for after they are given the Seal of God we are told:

> And after this I looked, and behold, a great multitude, which no one could count, from every nation and all tribes and peoples and tongues, standing before the throne and before the Lamb, clothed in white robes, and palm branches were in their hands...
>
> *(Revelation 7:9)*

What a harvest of souls—it will be so great that it will be impossible for an onlooker to count them!

Antichrist Invades the Temple

Now, perhaps the picture of the sequence of events becomes clearer to you.

Antichrist, all-powerful, has witnessed the stubborness of the believers who would rather be beheaded than accept the Mark. Those who have accepted the Mark have seen the believers starving, dying on the street. And this type of scene is occurring today.

I can remember when I visited Calcutta a couple years ago how the dust of that city seemed to hover over the streets in a cloud of death. I remember seeing at night the thousands of people lying on the street. They had no homes. Each morning a truck would pick up those who died of starvation and illnesses brought on by malnutrition during the night.

And this is the scene that Antichrist has witnessed. People would rather die than accept his Mark.

Then, to add insult to injury, suddenly the Jews whom he has protected by his treaty, start to become more unified with the erection of their Temple. He fears they will no longer rely on him.

And while others are accepting his Mark he discovers,

much to his amazement, that there are 144,000 Jews who have some type of divine mark on their foreheads as well — be it a visible or an invisible one. And, in defiance of his edicts, they are going about preaching that Christ alone can bring salvation to the world.

One can imagine the fiery wrath that erupts within him. To think that someone would challenge his sovereignty! No doubt he sends first a small police force to try to quell these evangelistic meetings held by individual members of the 144,000 Jews. What a surprise when he discovers that polite coercion will not work.

His anger rises. He sends his secret police to try and jeopardize the lives of these "sealed" Jews. But no form of threat becomes effective. Then he tells the police to kill any Jew preaching this "Christ-Gospel."

And the police come back and in amazement. Telling Antichrist that threats seem not to have any effect on them — and perhaps too, that even bullets do not seem to stop these zealots!

Finally, in desperation, he sends an entire army unit. But God's seal of protection is all-inclusive. Not one man, not one platoon, not one division...no, not even an entire army can silence these Jews who have been sealed in God's 144,000 missionary team!

Love knows no boundaries. The sign on the left warns that the border is behind, and that passage is forbidden. But the couple in the picture don't seem to care.

This fact, plus the stubborness of other believers, plus the growing power of Israel, leads Antichrist to make his most dastardly move, one that he hopes will once and for all crush the Jew and Israel. That move...to take over the Temple in Jerusalem.

Jerusalem, the Golden

During the captivity of the Jews under Nebuchadnezzar the Psalmist wrote a Psalm that would fit the situations of many centuries. Now again during this Tribulation Period, the message of this psalm again applies.

> By the rivers of Babylon,
> There we sat down and wept,
> When we remembered Zion...
>
> How can we sing the Lord's song
> In a foreign land?
> If I forget you, O Jerusalem,
> May my right hand forget her skill.
>
> May my tongue cleave to the roof of my mouth,
> If I do not remember you,
> If I do not exalt Jerusalem
> Above my chief joy...
>
> (Psalm 137:1,4-6)

And the Jews then did not forget Jerusalem. Then when in relative peace during the first 3½ years of the Tribulation, they were still rejoicing in their new Temple with the message of this Psalm seeming no longer to apply. They were unaware that sudden tragedy was to befall them!

Jerusalem, first and foremost is a city whose name means peace! Yet it has sadly been through the centuries a city of war, taken, lost, retaken nearly 50 times within 3000 years!

Israel, after 2000 years, finally achieved statehood in 1948. Yet their migration in reasonable numbers actually began in the 1880's. By 1882 there were some 25,000 Jews in Palestine, nearly all of them descended from the remnants of Palestine's two million Jews of Roman times.

The Birth of Zionism

Then, Theodor Herzl, born in Budapest in 1860, was to have an impact on the Jewish migration to Israel. At first,

Foreign Office,
November 2nd, 1917.

Dear Lord Rothschild,

I have much pleasure in conveying to you, on behalf of His Majesty's Government, the following declaration of sympathy with Jewish Zionist aspirations which has been submitted to, and approved by, the Cabinet

'His Majesty's Government view with favour the establishment in Palestine of a national home for the Jewish people, and will use their best endeavours to facilitate the achievement of this object, it being clearly understood that nothing shall be done which may prejudice the civil and religious rights of existing non-Jewish communities in Palestine, or the rights and political status enjoyed by Jews in any other country'.

I should be grateful if you would bring this declaration to the knowledge of the Zionist Federation.

Lord Balfour's
declaration of 1917.

Theodor Herzl,
founder of the
Zionist movement.

up until he was 34 years of age, he managed to avoid his Jewishness and the problems of the Jews. But, as a newspaper correspondent serving in Paris the ugliness of the Dreyfus court-martial aroused his interest.[1]

Herzl favored a self-governing Jewish republic but was content even to accept territory in Argentina or Africa if the state could not be built in Palestine. The first Zionist congress convened in August 1897. Two hundred delegates attended. Zionism was alive.[2]

Herzl wrote in his diary after the conference:

> At Basle, I found the Jewish State. If I were to say this today, I would be met by universal laughter. In five years perhaps and certainly in fifty, everyone will say it.

His predictions came true.

Within two years of its founding, the World Zionist Organization had 114,000 members! Herzl after many years of effort seemed to hit one roadblock after another. His heart was weak. Finally, in 1904 he went to Italy in hopes of making a Jewish state in North Africa. He died in July of that year at the age of 44. He never was to see the Promised Land.

But in 1948 Israel did become a state. And between 1948 and the outbreak of the 1967 War, American Jews poured over 1½ Billion Dollars into Israel. Baron Edmond de Rothschild and his friend in Paris raised $1,500,000 at a private party. In London, the baron's cousin, Lord Rothschild, gave a party of his own at which he contributed $2,800,000 to Israel and his 30 guests pledged another $17,000,000. The dream of Israel could only be built by the financial sacrifices of world Jewry.

Now the final agony of Jerusalem was about to begin.

The rabbis say:

---

[1] The Dreyfus affair, involved an Austrian Jew in the French army who was falsely charged with being a spy for Germany. It exposed the hatred against the Jew which still lingered in "democratic and enlightened" Europe.

[2] Zionism is the world-wide movement for the establishment in Palestine of a national homeland for the Jews.

Ten parts of beauty are allocated to the world by the Creator, and Jerusalem received nine of them.

But ten parts of suffering were allocated to the world and Jerusalem received nine; the world but one.

The victorious English troops enter Jerusalem. For the first time since the Crusades a non-Moslem army entered the Holy City in 1917.

General Allenby, the Commander-in-Chief of the British forces in Palestine, is ceremonially received at the entrance to Jerusalem in December, 1917.

Just one month prior, Lord Balfour, England's foreign minister, had accepted the principle of a Jewish national home in Palestine. Alongside the British soldiers who entered Jerusalem were units of the Jewish Legion which included a corporal: David Ben-Gurion!

It was Naftali Herz Imber who penned, **Hatikvah** ("The Hope"), Israel's national anthem.

So long as still within our breasts
    the Jewish heart beats true;
So long as still towards the East,
    to Zion, looks the Jew,
So long our hope is not yet lost —
    two thousand years we cherished it —
To live in freedom in the land
    of Zion and Jerusalem.

In an address in 1957, in a moving speech before the Trusteeship Council of the United Nations, Abba Eban, made this speech:

...The People of Israel and the Jewish people throughout the world are deeply inspired by the restoration of Israel's independent life in Jerusalem in fulfillment of ancient prophecy...

Our vision is of a Jerusalem wherein a free people develops its reviving institutions...Perhaps in this as in other critical periods of history, a free Jerusalem may proclaim redemption to mankind.

Redemption to mankind? This is exactly what Antichrist did not want...at least not a redemption that included God. For Antichrist, now imbued with power, imagines himself to be god.

And, at this point in time, as he prepares to force Israel to submit, his research has already made him aware of Jerusalem's past history. But what he will not accept is Jerusalem's future glory under Christ, the Messiah! And to this end, he will strive to change Bible prophecy!

Prepare Now to Shed Your Tears

This is the earthly New Jerusalem. The Dome of the Rock no longer dominates the sky. In its place stands a gleaming Temple, perhaps patterned after Ezekiel's Temple (Ezekiel chapters 40-48), or after Solomon's Temple, with its roof 180 feet high, paneled with cypress wood, plated with pure gold, inlaid with beautiful jewels.

Perhaps, like Solomon's Temple, the Holy of Holies will be overlaid with the finest gold worth over $18 million. Possibly 26 ounce gold nails will be used. Perhaps, at the front of the Temple will again be the ancient two pillars, each 52½ feet high.

And the altar...perhaps, like Solomon's Temple, it will be forged from bronze, 30 feet long, 30 feet wide and 15 feet high. There will be 10 gold lampstands, 10 tables. And, if they follow Solomon's plans, 100 solid gold bowls!

Can you in your mind's eye, imagine the ceremony as an Ark is again placed into the inner room of the Temple—the Holy of Holies—and set beneath the angel's wings.

The Ark, symbolizing the very presence of God! The most sacred object of the Temple!

And as Solomon, the chief Rabbi of Israel, or a newly consecrated High Priest, may intone the words:

> *The Lord has said that He would dwell in the thick cloud.*
>
> *I have built Thee a lofty house,*
> *And a place for Thy dwelling forever.*
> *(2 Chronicles 6:1-2)*

The treaty Antichrist made with Israel relaxed tensions between Israel and the Arabs. Annual expenditures for military preparedness now could be greatly diminished. At last money is available for the people and for their Temple.

The earlier War of Ezekiel 38:1-39:16 involving Russia may not have wiped out Russia entirely. In fact, Daniel 11:40—a difficult verse to interpret—may indicate that Russia, the "King of the North," at this time will challenge the treaty which Antichrist has made with Israel. This provides Antichrist not only with an opportunity to destroy this northern confederacy—Russia and her allies—but this war also will give Antichrist the opportunity now to fully take over Israel.

This middle of the seven years is often referred to as the "Abomination of Desolation" and it begins the last 3½ years known as the "Time of Jacob's Trouble" or the "**Great** Tribulation (Jeremiah 30:7; Matthew 24:15,21; Daniel 9: 27).

There are four groups within Israel with whom Antichrist

will enter into conflict:

1. Jews who will not yield to accept the Mark;
2. Redeemed Jews who accept the Messiah as Lord;
3. The 144,000, of which some reside in Jerusalem;
4. The Two Witnesses (See Revelation 11:3-5).

The prophet, Daniel, even in Old Testament days, could see the agony that Israel would suffer, when he wrote:

...there shall be a time of trouble such as never was since there was a nation...

(Daniel 12:1)

The Dawn of Destruction

The following, written in the form of a NOVEL, is a reflection on what might occur on that awesome day.

Dawn dilutes the dark over the city of Jerusalem. It is the Sabbath Day. The first streams of sunlight dance gaily on the golden cupola of the Temple. Slowly, the city of Jerusalem wakes up to a new day little realizing its import.

The skyline appears with its multitudes of domes, minarets, spires and towers. The orthodox East European Jews, in their own quarters, quickly brush their beards and side curls, put on their silk kaftans and don their fur-brimmed hats. This is the Sabbath and they must be ready.

Down the cobbled lanes and cramped courtyards, they start to come, heading towards the Temple.

The Old City, pierced by eight gateways, is beginning to awake as well. Roosters are crowing their announcement of the morning. The Jews make their way through the winding, narrow streets of the Old City. The smell of pastry shops still mingles with the smell of donkeys and of lambs being brought to slaughter. Beyond the site of what once was the Holy Sepulcher are modern, expensive shops selling silk and brocaded fabrics, shoes and jewelry.

And higher than the surrounding mountains of Moab and Judea, here is Mount Moriah, where since the beginning of time has lured man in quest of faith and sacrifice.

Streams of endless craving, clinging, dreaming, flowing

This could well be the scene! Antichrist entering Jerusalem with an armada of tanks.

Russian rocket launchers follow.

day and night...midnights, years, decades, centuries, streams of tears have been waiting for this great day... the Sabbath once again in the Temple in Jerusalem.

The quiet noises that spell security, the bells, the urging prodding of the donkeys, the Moslem call to worship, the honking of horns...suddenly all stop!

From a distance can be heard the sound of drums. A whistle is blown so shrill it seems to vibrate the marrow of one's bones!

Then the sound of a band penetrates the still calmness of that Jerusalem Sabbath morning. The music is not one of peace. It is a March Militaire.

Anyone living in Jerusalem, or for that matter anywhere in the world, would recognize that March as easily as he would recognize his own son. It is the March of Antichrist. His national anthem. It was the March that blared away incessantly as people lined up to receive the Mark.

It was the March that Antichrist had played as he entered into battle with nation after nation.

And with the triple trills, it was the March that was played in his triumphal return from victory.

It was heard many times.

No one could deny that sound.

It was the sound of fury. It was the sound of victory. It was the sound that made people cringe in fear. It was the sound of power...a miracle power that seemed to overtake even God.

It was the sound that came as a Saviour, but was soon known as a Slayer.

Now, in the quiet Sabbath dawn in Jerusalem, down the old Jericho road, past the Church of All Nations and the Garden of Gethsemane, the marching band gets louder. The cadenced march of soldiers can be heard as well as the clacking of horses in military precision.

Now the city of Jerusalem is fully awake. Like a bolt of lightening the message of the marching army has filtered through every closeted door.

There had been rumors that something drastic would pierce the calm of Jerusalem...but they were only rumors.

And the countenance of Antichrist, though fierce, did not seem to betray his true intentions.

The Leaders of Israel had assured their people that this man was the one man who had integrity. He meant what he said. This was a Treaty that would not be broken. His word was almost as good as the word of God! Yet there was enough people who knew history's course to cause a curtain of doubt to spread over the populace.

And now, it appeared that all doubts would be fully materialized in great tragedy and dismay.

Where was Antichrist headed?

A phlanx of cars...big black, bubbletopped limousines... followed after the band. Running alongside were well-dressed secret service men with one hand on their hip, ready to pull their laser guns at the least hint of trouble.

Crowds now filled the curbs to overflowing. But specially-trained soldiers bordered the streets locked arm in arm. Anyone trying to cross the street was cruelly pushed back or knocked to the ground, many unconscious from the blow.

A near hysteria engulfed the crowd as they witnessed the scene.

Where could Antichrist be headed?

The whole crowd seemed to ask the question. But the soldiers, stern-faced would not reply.

Suddenly, one bystander spotted a familiar face in the long line of limousines. It was a Jew...a turncoat Jew, who sacrificed his beliefs in Judaism to become a member of the Cabinet of Antichrist. He could not conceal his secret.

Someone in the crowd who knew him, shouted, "Where are you going?"

Before he could catch his tongue, he quickly replied, "TO THE TEMPLE."

Like a wave "TO THE TEMPLE" rippled down the sea of faces until it engulfed them in a bath of tears and sorrow.

What they had feared for years was now becoming a reality ...in their own lifetime!

Quickly dedicated Jews managed to rush to the Temple. They made a human wall blocking the entrance.

But the soldiers had already anticipated this move. Within a short time every Jew in the wall had been massacred and cleared away even before the disturbance had a chance to reach the eyes of Antichrist.

It was the Sabbath. No dedicated Jew would fight on this holy day. Antichrist knew this.

Antichrist with his entourage proceeded up the Temple steps. Behind him soldiers carried an object of unusual size, covered by a shroud.

They ascended up to the porch and headed towards the Holy of Holies. Above them, if they cared to look, was cemented in place anew the ancient inscription forbidding Gentiles to enter the inner court of the Temple on the pain of death.

> No stranger is to enter within the balustrade around the temple and enclosure. Whoever is caught will be responsible to himself for his death, which will ensue.

This threat did not stop them!

This could well be the scene when Antichrist enters the Temple area in Jerusalem.

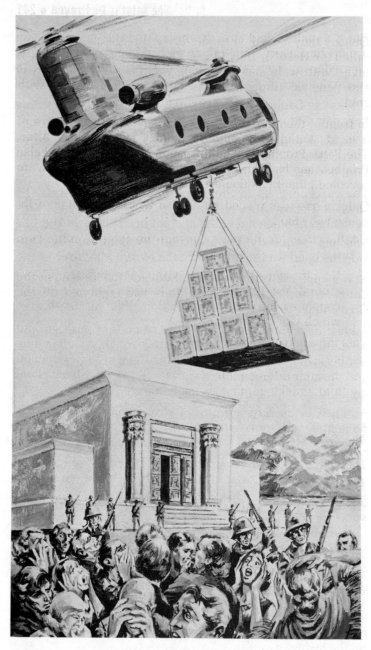

A huge helicopter crane suddenly came into position and its giant tentacles grasped the Altar roughly and in one grating swoop lifted it up to the sky.

Quickly they moved on to the forward large main chamber called the **Hekal** or Holy Place. The Holy Place, about 45 ft. high, 30 ft. wide and 60 ft. long was floored with cypress and panelled throughout the cedar, lavishly inlaid with gold.

In front of them lay the Altar of Incense. With the wave of a hand, Antichrist's soldiers quickly removed the Altar. The False Prophet looked on, smiling approval. The False Prophet then had the shroud uncovered. Two statues were revealed...identical likenesses of Antichrist.

Quickly one was placed on a base where the Altar of Incense had stood.

And just as quickly, the group left, walking rapidly. Outside the band was again playing the March Militaire.

Now a huge crowd had gathered outside the Temple at the Court of the Priests. Here, soldiers had cordoned off the Great Altar.

A huge helicopter crane suddenly came into position and its giant tentacles grasped the Altar roughly and in one grating swoop lifted it up to the sky. The giant jaws opened and the altar dropped into a very large truck with a sickening thud, cracking into a thousand pieces!

And just as quickly, a group of strong soldiers, eased the remaining statue of Antichrist off a specially constructed lift and onto the space where once the Great Altar stood.

The False Prophet commanded that everyone kneel in obeisance as Antichrist made his way to his armored car.

Suddenly someone in the crowd shouted in a cry of unbearable tragedy:

IT'S THE ABOMINATION OF DESOLATION!
Oh, Israel, my Israel!
Jerusalem the Golden is Lost
THE MESSIAH HAS FORGOTTEN HIS PEOPLE!

There was no stopping now. The whole city erupted as one in a mournful cry. Their Temple had been prostituted by the swine of sin.

A Judas once again had betrayed them.

There would be no peace in Jerusalem.

Robbed of their Temple by the actions of Antichrist, Jews may flock to the Wailing Wall, holding umbrellas as a symbol of their sorrow.

Israel would no more be a nation. Someone greater than a Pharaoh, someone greater than a Nebuchadnezzar, someone greater than an Alexander the Great, greater than a Titus or a Hadrian or a Hitler, had destroyed the very hope of Israel.

The City of Peace was now a city of desecration.

The God of the Holy of Holies had not yet saved His people.

All the hopes of all the years, in one day, were swallowed in bitter defeat.

It was the Day Israel Dies!

13

TRAGEDY AND TRIUMPH

All the hopes of all the years are suddenly shattered. The cries of anguish flood the city of Jerusalem.

And within moments Telstar had beamed the news worldwide and instant replays on television screens again re-enact the horror that took place at the Temple.

But it is not depicted as a horror. The announcers are careful to say that "...some disloyal dissident Jews created the disturbance that unfortunately resulted in the death of bystanders."

Now full scale tragedy will begin. No longer will the Temple be used for sacrifice to God. Instead it shall become·a blasphemy of worship directed to Antichrist himself.

Antichrist, virtually the leader of the entire world, had quashed the opposition. Nothing can stand in his way now, so he believes.

Many Jews cry out:

> How can the God of Jacob, of Isaac allow such suffering to be inflicted on His people?

At last...the Jew is again crying out to their God. Their hearts are again becoming softened and the answer seems all too clear. For centuries His people have, along with the rest of the world, gone their own way, relying on earthly gods from the Golden Calf of Moses' day to the liberal teachings of the modern day. Buoyed by the lightening victory of the Six Day War many began to rely on their own might, their own knowledge and not on God.

And now, in the midst of their suffering, they begin to realize that God permitted the abomination of their Temple... the one thing they held sacred...to bring them to an attitude where they would see Christ as their Messiah. At last they are beginning to see the difference between the cross-clad Crusaders who killed Jews and the cross laden Saviour who still calls them to trust in Him.

But tragedy still lies ahead of the Jew!

Two Thirds to Die

Hundreds upon hundreds of years ago the prophet Zechariah wrote:

> And it will come about in all the land, declares the Lord, That two parts in it will be cut off and perish; But the third will be left in it.
> (Zechariah 13:8)

Think of it. What a casualty list!

Zechariah says that two thirds of Israel will be killed! Does he mean that two thirds will perish and only one-third survive beginning with the time of Christ's death (Zechariah 13:7, the previous verse)? Or does the Prophet speak entirely of an end-time slaughter? We hope not; time alone will tell. Christ, however, calls this period, a time of "Great tribulation such as was not since the beginning of the world..." (Matthew 24:21). Undoubtedly synagogues, too, will be destroyed en masse. Perhaps Antichrist will try to better the record of the Roman emperor Vespasian, who destroyed 480 synagogues in the Holy Land.

The Flight to the Wilderness

Some Jews, eager to save their lives, may compromise their stand and follow Antichrist. They may even betray their own loved ones so they may escape the wrath of this world leader.

Many in Israel, however, will be true. They will refuse to compromise their position, refuse to bow the knee to Antichrist. But such refusal will mean death if they continue in Jerusalem. Therefore comes the necessity for them to flee as quickly as possible out of that city. It is as though once again Pharaoh's army is pursuing the Hebrew children to the Red Sea.

The compassion of Jesus, the Messiah, is revealed in his prophecy in Matthew 24:21-22:

> ...there will be a great tribulation, such as has not occurred since the beginning of the world until now, nor ever shall.
>
> And unless those days had been cut short, no life would have been saved; but for the sake of the elect those days shall be cut short.

These verses tell us two important things:

> 1. This tribulation terror reigned on the Jews at this time will be the greatest tribulation they have ever passed through...surpassing all other trials!
>
> 2. And, if these days of terror were not cut short, no Jew would remain alive!

But God has a plan and His plan and purpose will always be fulfilled to the letter.

Revelation 12 reveals the fact that Satan is behind this persecution of Israel, as he has always been. Why? Because he knew that Israel would produce the Messiah, and because he desires to frustrate God's sworn eventual plans of grace and salvation toward Abraham's children of promise, the Jews.

The Urgency of Departure

Jesus Christ in Matthew 24:15-18 warns the people of Israel:

> Therefore when you see the ABOMINATION OF DESOLATION which was spoken of through Daniel the prophet, standing in the holy place...
>
> then let those who are in Judea flee to the mountains;
>
> let him who is in the field not turn back to get his cloak.

The urgency of immediate flight to the wilderness is stressed here. How often in a fire, someone will rush back into the burning house to get a pet canary or his wallet...only to die in the attempt!

Christ foretold over two thousand years ago that when Antichrist desecrates the Temple in Jerusalem...the Jews must *immediately* leave the city and head towards the wilderness.

There, the faithful remnant of Israel will be fed and protected by their Messiah, just as He protected them in the Wilderness en route to the Promised Land of Canaan. Only this time their Promised Land will be eternal and complete.

> And the two wings of the great eagle were given to the woman, in order that she might fly into the wilderness to her place, where she was nourished for atime and times and half a time [3½ years], from the presence of the serpent [Satan and Antichrist].
>
> *(Revelation 12:14)*

This prophecy was made before the time of Christ through the prophet, Zechariah:

> And I will bring the third part through the fire,
> Refine them as silver is refined,
> And test them as gold is tested.
> They will call on My name,
> And I will answer them;
> I will say, "They are My people."
> And they will say, "The Lord is my God."
>
> *(Zechariah 13:9)*

Can you fully grasp the significance of the last two lines? Read them over again once more...this time slowly and carefully.

On the Mount of Olives in Jerusalem, Jesus Christ, in anguish at one time cried:

> O Jersalem, Jerusalem, who kills the prophets and stones those who are sent to her!
>
> How often I wanted to gather your children together the way a hen gathers her chicks under her wings, and you were unwilling!
>
> *(Matthew 23:37)*

UNWILLING!

Unwilling to leave the leeks and the garlic of Egypt, unwilling to follow Moses, unwilling to offer perfect sacrifices to God, unwilling to follow the Law, unwilling to avoid mixed marriages with unbelievers, unwilling to give God His full tithes and offerings, unwilling to keep a clean heart, unwilling to expose and admit their sin.

Petra, presently in Jordan, may be the place of refuge where thousands of Jews may flee during the persecutions of the Tribulation Period.

God, in Malachi 1:6-3:15 lists 32 sins the people of Israel were guilty of, from dishonoring God to offering polluted bread on the altar and working wickedness.

For centuries...2000 years, we as Christians believe that the people of Israel have been unwilling to acknowledge their Messiah.

But now, hungry, shivering and exhausted from their flight from Jerusalem and their flight from the enemy down through the ages...finally, God's Plan of Love is fulfilled.

Finally God says to them:

They are My people!

And all thc Jews that are left...one-third of them, reply:

The Lord is my God!

The long road of trials and tribulations is about to end. The nightmare of the past is about to become the triumph of tomorrow!

The sounds of war will be everywhere as nations gird for the final conflict at Armageddon.

The only Middle East area not in this conflict, it appears to me, will be the land of Edom, Moab and Ammon, which are all located in present-day Jordan.

Where do the Jews flee?

The Bible says in Zechariah 14:5:

And you will flee by the valley of My mountains...
Then the Lord, my God, will come, and all the
holy ones with Him!

There are some who have suggested that the area where the Jews will flee is the rock city of Petra. Petra, once called "the rainbow city" because of its various hues of color in the stone, had 267,000 inhabitants. It was a large market center at the junction of a great caravan route, Now, however, except for a few nomads, it is desolate.

The city is inaccessible except through the gorge or canyon in the mountains. This opening is wide enough for only two horses abreast. The perpendicular walls of this gorge are from 400 to 700 feet high. The existing buildings in Petra are cut from the solid rock in the mountain...and they still stand today! Even a clear spring bubbles over these rose-red rocks and wild figs grow on the banks.

It is quite possible that Petra could be the city that the Jews flee to, although the Scriptures do not supply such detailed information in this prophecy. We do know, however, that they will flee into some area or chaotic region which the Bible calls, "the wilderness" and we also know that God will here protect them when Antichrist tries to destroy them.

Antichrist, in fury, it would appear, tries to flood out the hiding place where the Jews are secluded.

> And the serpent poured water like a river out of his mouth after the woman, so that he might cause her to be swept away with the flood.
>
> (Revelation 12:15)

Now, whether this speaks of a literal flood of water or means that Antichrist will mount a vicious propaganda campaign to discredit the Jew, or that he will launch a flood of greater persecution...only time can tell. I would be inclined to believe he will do all three.

But for these last 3½ years, the Jew will be protected from anihilation by God until the end of the Tribulation Period.

Satan Thrown Out of Heaven

During this final 3½ years something very dramatic occurs. Satan is evicted from Heaven! Here's what occurs:

> ...there was war in heaven, Michael and his angels waging war with the Dragon [Satan].
>
> And the dragon and his angels waged war, and they were not strong enough, and there was no longer a place found for them in heaven.
>
> And the great dragon was thrown down, the serpent of old who is called the devil and Satan, who deceives the whole world; he was thrown down to the earth, and his angels were thrown down with him.
>
> (Revelation 12:7-9)

Satan is identified as the deceiver of the whole earth. Up until now he could create havoc over the entire earth from his place in Heaven. At last finally he is evicted by Michael and his angels.

Michael is an archangel and is the prince and guardian over the destinies of the nation Israel. See Daniel 10:21 and 12:1.

With Satan being cast from Heaven, one can imagine his bitterness. And this bitterness will be vented in full force upon Israel, particularly upon the believing Jew.

Now, as mentioned earlier, Satan, tries to flood out those Jews (the 1/3rd) that are hiding in the wilderness.

In reading Revelation 12:16, however, it would appear that an earthquake or some unusual event occurs that opens the earth causing the flood waters not to flow into the area where the Jews are hiding...but rather to be diverted. This, of course, may be a figure to show us that God will cause the flood of evil poured out by Satan against the Jew to be somehow absorbed—perhaps in an internal rebellion

Air view of the Euphrates River showing its great circuitous, treeless course. One day, during the Tribulation Period, 200 million Asians will cross the River Euphrates and kill a third of mankind. See Revelation 9:13-19.

against Antichrist.

So enraged does Satan become at this, that he makes war on every true believer upon which he can lay his hands.

The Rape of Jerusalem

During this time Antichrist, who has set up Headquarters in Jerusalem, runs rampant through the city.

For a more comprehensive view of what will occur in the ensuing Battle of Armageddon, we suggest that you read GUIDE TO SURVIVAL and WHAT IN THE WORLD WILL HAPPEN NEXT?, both by Salem Kirban.

But briefly, the nations of the world will converge towards Jerusalem. The major powers will prepare for the biggest battle ever imagined.

Antichrist will get wind of a tremendous army proceeding from the Orient. Some 200 million troops marching towards Israel, possibly with the intent of themselves destroying Jerusalem and taking over world rulership from Antichrist (Revelation 9:14-16; 16:12,14).

In his fury, Antichrist will himself call upon his vast forces for an attack against Jerusalem. And Zechariah prophesies:

> I will gather all the nations against Jerusalem to battle, and the city will be captured, the houses plundered, the women ravished, and half of the city exiled...
>
> (Zechariah 14:2)

Antichrist, employing techniques of clever military maneuver, seeks to choose his own battlefield to meet the oncoming Asiatic army of China, possibly in coalition with Japan and other Southeast Asian powers.

He desires to fight on a battleground that will be to his advantage. Therefore, he sets himself up in the mountains of Judea where he will have natural defenses. The area... the valley of Jezreel...the Plains of Esdraelon...known as Armageddon!

The Battle of Armageddon

Antichrist, with his western confederacy of nations, prepares to battle the Asiatic force.

But suddenly the heavens open. With perhaps an awesome

silence, the sky appears to roll back as a scroll. The two opposing sides, who had been firing at each other, suddenly realize they have an even greater foe...THE KING OF KINGS, THE LORD OF LORDS.

Now a phenomenal occurrence takes place directed by God Himself! The Lord Jesus Christ comes down from the Heavens on a white horse with the armies of heaven following. All are dressed in the finest white linen and also seen to be riding on white horses.

The prophecies in Revelation describe this scene most vividly:

> And I saw heaven opened; and behold, a white horse, and He who sat upon it is called Faithful and True; and in righteousness He judges and wages war.
>
> And His eyes are a flame of fire, and upon His head are many diadems; and He has a name written upon Him which no one knows except Himself.
>
> And He is clothed with a robe dipped in blood; and His name is called The Word of God.
>
> And the armies which are in heaven, clothed in fine linen, white and clean, were following Him on white horses.
>
> And from His mouth comes a sharp sword, so that with it He may smite the nations; and He will rule them with a rod of iron; and He treads the wine press of the fierce wrath of God, the Almighty.
>
> And on His robe and on His thigh He has a name written, "KING OF KINGS, AND LORD OF LORDS."
>
> *(Revelation 19:11-16)*

Even David foresaw this culmination of the events of history when he penned the Second Psalm. Spoken centuries before the actual occurrence of the Battle of Armageddon will occur, the prophet David sees the nations of the earth in rebellion against God which reaches its climax under the rulership of Antichrist. Here in David's writing the world powers finalized in Antichrist declare that they will

The Battle of Armageddon! The Lord Jesus Christ comes down from the Heavens on a white horse with the armies of heaven following.

not permit God to set up his King on David's throne to reign over the world.

God actually laughs at the vain boasting of Antichrist and we read in Psalm 2:1-6 that He quietly sits on His throne in Heaven and chuckles.

The opposing armies...the armies of the Orient and the armies of Antichrist...realizing that some startling occurrence is taking place directed by God, decide it is time to unite forces in order to devote all their energies into fighting the Lord Jesus Christ.

What happens?

The combined forces of the armies of the world with all their armed nuclear power are destroyed by a direct judgment from God.

Thus, the Battle of Armageddon which began amid the struggles of the revived Roman empire with the Antichrist at its head, and his rivals, the Oriental kings from the east ...is climaxed with a united battle of the Satanic hordes against the Lord.

The words of Scripture tell us what occurs during God's final judgments:

> And the seventh angel poured out his bowl upon the air; and a loud voice came out of the temple from the throne saying, "It is done."
>
> And there were flashes of lightning and sounds and peals of thunder; and there was a great earthquake, such as there had not been since man came to be upon the earth, so great an earthquake as it, and so mighty.
>
> And the great city was split into three parts, and the cities of the nations fell...
>
> And every island fled away, and the mountains were not found.
>
> And huge hailstones, about 100 pounds each, came down from heaven upon men; and men blasphemed God because of the plague of the hail...
>
> (Revelation 16:17-21)
>
> And I saw an angel standing in the sun; and he cried out with a loud voice, saying to all the birds which fly in mid-heaven, "Come, assemble for the great supper of God; in order that you may eat the flesh of kings and the flesh of commanders and the flesh of mighty men and the flesh of horses and of those who sit on them and the flesh of all men...
>
> And I saw the beast [Antichrist] and the kings of the earth and their armies, assembled to make war against Him who sat upon the horse and against His [God's] army.
>
> (Revelation 19:17-19)

Here we see at the onset of the Battle of Armageddon that God's full judgment falls on those who have opposed him, the forces of Antichrist and the armies of the world. So great is the destruction that an earthquake occurs which the Scriptures tell us will be the greatest earthquake the world has ever experienced!

Millions Die

The three greatest earthquakes the world has experienced up to now were:

1556 AD	Shensi, China	830,000 dead
1737 AD	Calcutta, India	300,000 dead
1920 AD	Kansu, China	180,000 dead

And this earthquake that occurs during the Battle of Armageddon brings a death toll and destruction greater than the world has ever experienced! Imagine hailstones falling that weigh about 100 pounds (Revelation 16:21). What gaping holes will be left in the earth as the tremendous forces of such accelerating weights plummet to the ground!

The destruction to the wicked armies at Armageddon is complete. Over 200 million men die. The birds are released by God to come and feast on the lifeless bodies of man and horse alike (Revelation 19:17-18).

We are told that the blood bath of Armageddon is so great and so devastating that the length of over 185 miles of Israel is splattered by this blood bath! See Revelation 14:20.

Antichrist Meets His Waterloo

Daniel, centuries before, had seen what would occur at the Battle of Armageddon:

> And he [Antichrist] will pitch the tents of his royal pavilion between the seas and the beautiful Holy Mountain; yet he will come to his end, and no one will help him.
>
> (Daniel 11:45)

Between Jerusalem and the sea, Antichrist will erect his special Headquarters.

But, in the heat of the Battle of Armageddon, when God slays the armies of man, there will be no one to help Antichrist.

No one! Because no one will exist who **can** help him. What humiliation! Satan's counterfeit ruler, who up to this moment was self-sufficient, suddenly will find himself totally incapable to help himself as he meets his Waterloo.

Not even his associate, the False Prophet, the religious leader of that age...not even he can help when both come face to face with God!

Revelation 19:20-21 tells us what happens:

> And the beast [Antichrist] was seized, and with
> him the false prophet who performed the signs in
> his presence, by which he deceived those who
> had received the mark of the beast and those
> who had worshipped his image; the two were
> thrown alive into the lake of fire which burns
> with brimstone.
>
> And the rest were killed with the sword which
> came from the mouth of Him who sat upon the
> horse, and all the birds were filled with their
> flesh.

Here where Deborah and Barak defeated the Canaanites
(Judges 4,5), here where Gideon defeated the Midianites
(Judges 7), here where David defeated Goliath (1 Samuel
17), here God will once-and-for-all defeat not only Antichrist and the False Prophet, but also the instigator of sin
into the world . . . SATAN.

> ...I saw an angel descending from heaven; he was
> holding the key of the abyss — the bottomless
> pit — and a great chain was in his hand.
>
> And he gripped and overpowered the dragon, that
> old serpent of old, who is the devil and Satan,
> and bound him for a thousand years...
> *(Revelation 20:1-2)*

With the exception of the flapping of wings and the chirp-
ing of the birds, the battlefield is quiet now. The stench of
death is still everywhere.

The time of the Gentiles has come to a close.

Antichrist and the False Prophet are actually cast **alive**
into the Lake of Fire without awaiting any final judgment.
Their destiny is the place of eternal suffering burning
with brimstone, a place of perpetual darkness with no hope
of deliverance.

Satan, at this time, is bound in the bottomless pit for 1000
years. He is not permitted to reappear until the end of the
Millennium Period.

The Day Israel is Judged

The next event that occurs before the 1000 year Millennium

Judgment of living Israel will possibly take place in the desert at Kadesh-Barnea. Money will not be able to buy eternal life!

begins is the Judgment of the Nation Israel.

This judgment occurs after the Battle of Armageddon and before the Millennium. This is a time when all **living** people of Jewish heritage will be judged.

The place of judgment will be on earth. All living Israel will be regathered, possibly at Kadesh-Barnea or at some similar location. Kadesh-Barnea is about 65 miles south of Gaza in the Negev desert.

It is here that the Israelites spent many years after their exodus from Egypt.

What will happen here? Malachi 3:2-5 speaks of the Lord's judgment being as a refiner's fire that will purify and purge living Israel. God will judge each individual, separating the saved from the unsaved.

The unsaved, those who are not believers, will be cut-off and cast into Hell (Ezekiel 20:37 and Matthew 25:30).

The saved, those who have accepted Jesus Christ as their Messiah, will be taken into the 1000 year Millennium as Living Believers. These Jews will be resettled in Jerusalem and the Promised Land and will reign with the Lord Jesus Christ forever.

This is the glorious day in Israel's history. This is the fulfillment of the new covenant, of which both Ezekiel and Jeremiah spoke—

> Behold, days are coming, declares the Lord, "when I will make a new covenant with the house of Israel and with the house of Judah,
>
> not like the covenant which I made with their fathers in the day I took them by the hand to bring them out of the land of Egypt, My covenant which they broke, although I was a husband to them," declares the Lord.
>
> "But this is the covenant which I will make with the house of Israel after those days...I will put My law within them, and on their heart I will write it; and I will be their God, and they shall be My people...for I will forgive their iniquity, and their sin I will remember no more."
>
> (Jeremiah 31:31-34)

And through the prophet Ezekiel come even further promises:

> I will take you from the nations, gather you from all the lands, and bring you into your own land.
>
> Then I will sprinkle clean water on you, and you will be clean; I will cleanse you from all your filthiness and from all your idols.
>
> Moreover, I will give you a new heart and put a new spirit within you; and I will remove the heart of stone from your flesh and give you a heart of flesh.
>
> And I will put My Spirit within you and cause you to walk in My statutes, and you will be careful to observe My ordinances.
>
> "And you will live in the land that I gave to your forefathers; so you will be My people, and I will be your God."
>
> *(Ezekiel 36:24-28)*

The days of Israel's suffering and spiritual blindness will be over! The times of the persecutions of Antichrist are finished. The long-awaited Messiah of Israel has again come!

He, whom Israel rejected in his First Coming some 2000 years ago, will be accepted as Messiah in his Second Coming to earth at the end of the Battle of Armageddon.

The Nation of Israel is Born!

The nation of Israel, under the banner of God, will be born in one day...one glorious day.

In the 1000 year Millennium Israel by virtue of her homeland will be exalted above the nations (Isaiah 14:1,2; 49: 22,23; 60:14-17).

Israel will become God's witness during the Millennium (Isaiah 44:8; 61:6; Zechariah 4:1-7; 8:3).

The Lord Jesus Christ will be King, and it appears that David will be some type of vice-regent (Jeremiah 30:9; Ezekiel 34:23; Hosea 3:5).

Palestine will be redistributed among the twelve tribes of Israel during the Millennium. Seven tribes will occupy the northern area and five the southern area.

Between these two areas there is a section of ground set apart for the Lord. It appears that this hallowed ground will be akin to a spacious square 34 miles each way or about 1160 square miles. Here will be the center of divine government and worship. The Temple, the Millennial Temple, will be located in Jerusalem, in the center of this area of Holy Oblation, upon the heights of the city's holy elevation. See Isaiah 2:4, Micah 4:1-4 and Ezekiel 37:26.

The sons of the line of Zadok will again be assigned the priestly duties (Ezekiel 40:46; 43:19; 44:15; 48:11).

You may remember that Zadok was the high priest in David's time who was loyal to the King.

Ezekiel, in chapters 40-48, is strangely silent on some key items of the Temple. This may well mean that in the coming Temple they will be absent: For example:

The Final Temple will perhaps have no veil nor will it have a table of showbread. This will not be needed since Christ the Living Bread will be present.

There may be no lampstands since Christ will be the Light.

There may be no ark of the Covenant since the Shekinah Glory himself will hover over all the world, as the glory cloud once did over the ark.

The East Gate may remain closed. You will recall it was from the eastern gate that the glory of God departed for the last time in the Old Testament (Ezekiel 10:18,19). Therefore in the act of keeping this Gate sealed, God may remind all those within that His glory will never again depart from His people (Ezekiel 44:1-3).

Israel can finally rejoice and God will delegate to Israel the opportunity to become His emissaries to the entire Millennial (1000 year) world.

Thus, in the Millennial Kingdom, Israel will once again be reunited as a nation. And Israel will be exalted even above the nations in this period!

> *The sons of those who afflicted you shall come bending low to you, and all those who despised you shall bow down at your feet...*
>
> *(Isaiah 60:14)*

In fact, in the Millennium, Israel with Egypt and Assyria will form a Messianic League living in peace!

> In that day Israel shall be the third with Egypt and with Assyria, a blessing in the midst of the earth.

> Whom the Lord of hosts has blessed, saying, Blessed be Egypt My people, and Assyria the work of My hands, and Israel My heritage.
>
> *(Isaiah 19:19-25)*

What a picture!

Down through the centuries God's people, the Jews, have yearned to be at peace in the Promised Land.

And down through the centuries from the Egyptians to the Assyrians, from the Babylonians to the Medes and Persians, from the rulers of Greece to the Romans, they have known nothing but tears and suffering.

The day will come when a believing Israel will rejoice!

These were the days...the long century years of days...the days when Israel died.

And when Antichrist desecrated the very Temple of God... this capstone of infamy was The Day Israel Died!

But through the agony of bitter defeat, God, in His infinite mercy provided a Way. That Way is the Messiah.

And the day will come when a believing Israel will rejoice, never again to know the sting of death, but rather, to experience the Day of Eternal Life! Thus the Apostle Paul 2000 years ago declared.

> *For I do not want you, brethren, to be uninformed of this mystery, lest you be wise in your own estimation, that a partial hardening has happened to Israel until the fulness of the Gentiles has come in; and thus all Israel will be saved; just as it is written,*
>
> *"THE DELIVERER WILL COME FROM ZION, HE WILL REMOVE UNGODLINESS FROM JACOB.*
> *AND THIS IS MY COVENANT WITH THEM, WHEN I TAKE AWAY THEIR SINS."*
>
> *From the standpoint of the gospel they are enemies for your sake, but from the standpoint of God's choice they are beloved for the sake of the fathers; for the gifts and the calling of God are irrevocable.*
>
> *(Romans 11:25-29)*

As the great Jewish poet, Jehuda Halevi wrote:

> O City of the World, beauteous in proud splendour!
> Oh, that I had eagle's wings that I might fly to thee,
> Till I wet thy dust with my tears!

That day will come! And the tears will be tears of fulfilled rejoicing!

THE END

WHAT WILL I DO WITH MY MESSIAH?

Will I reject Jesus as my Messiah because so many of my people have in the past rejected him?...Paul believed in him, and he was a rabbinical student. James and John, Peter and Andrew, believed on him, and they were Jewish, and from Israel no less. Besides, Isaiah the Prophet wrote of the Messiah, "He is despised and rejected of men" (Isa. 53:3).

Will I reject Jesus as my Messiah because of what some have done through the ages while wearing crosses?...Crusaders often killed Jewish people as did the Inquisition, the Nazis and the Communists. Medieval clerics made Jewish people wear badges and live in ghettoes. Yet Christ speaks against both hatred and murder, and upon the cross said, "Forgive them, Father, for they know not what they do." So too, Christians in many European countries risked their lives, and sometimes lost them, in order to hide and protect Jewish people from the Nazis. Clearly the perfections of Christ—this one who was born a Jew and who died with the writing above his cross, "King of the Jews"—are not to be confused with the wickedness of false Christians who contradict everything for which Christ stood. The imposter does not cancel out the true. Christ said, "I am the true vine" (John 15:1).

Will I reject Jesus as my Messiah because some say that no one can pay for any other person's sin, and besides it is not even necessary?...Yet Isaiah the Prophet wrote, "But he was wounded for our transgressions, he was bruised for our iniquities; the punishment for our peace was upon him, and with his stripes we are healed" (Isa. 53:5).

Will I reject Jesus as my Messiah because there have been many false messiahs and Jesus might be another of these? ...Yet all of the other messianic candidates put together have not produced for either the world or Jewry even one good proverb. In contrast to this, one need only read the New Testament gospel accounts to discover that everything that Jesus said was God honoring, remarkable, and holy. Jesus said, "If any man will do his (God's) will, he shall know of the teaching, whether it be of God, or whether I speak of myself" (John 7:17).

But, perhaps you heard it said by someone that Jesus never claimed to be the Messiah, he simply was a devout rabbi with new ideas?...Jesus said, "I am the light of the world" (John 8:12), "I am that bread of life" (John 6:48), and "I am the resurrection and the life; he that believeth in me, though he may die, yet shall he live" (John 11:25). These are not merely rabbinical claims; these are messianic claims!

Will you not try this one who said in Galilee.

> Come unto me,
> all ye that labor and are heavy laden,
> and I will give you rest
>
> (Matthew 11:28)

WHAT WILL YOU DO WITH JESUS?

Will you state that He never existed?

Will you simply say that He was a good man who did good things...like many other good men?

Will you say His message is not relevant to our enlightened age?

Your decision should not be based on what your friends or relatives say or do not say...or on your own private concept of heaven or hell. These really, in the final analysis, do not matter!

What is important...and what will govern your tomorrow in ETERNITY...is WHAT DOES THE BIBLE SAY? In light of God's standards, set forth in the Bible, your final destiny will be determined.

You can, as many do, simply choose to ignore Christ and the Scriptures...go on living your life, doing the best you know how to meet your problems, work to provide an income for your family, set aside a nest egg for retirement...

But THEN WHAT?

What happens when it comes time for you to depart from this earth?

Then WHAT WILL YOU DO WITH JESUS?

It takes NO DECISION on your part to go to Hell!

It **does** take a DECISION on your part, however, to go to Heaven!

> He that believeth on Him is not condemned: but he that believeth not is condemned already, because he hath not believed in the name of the only begotten Son of God.
>
> (John 3:18)

Whether you are Jew or Gentile, here are five basic observations in the Bible of which you should be aware:

1. ALL SINNED

> For all have sinned and come short of the glory of God.
>
> (Romans 3:23)

2. ALL LOVED

> For God so loved the world, that He gave His only begotten Son, that whosoever believeth in Him should not perish, but have everlasting life.
>
> (John 3:16)

3. ALL RAISED

> Marvel not at this: for the hour is coming, in which all that are in the graves shall hear his voice.
>
> And shall come forth; they that have done good, unto the resurrection of life; and they that have done evil, unto the resurrection of damnation.
>
> (John 5:28,29)

4. ALL JUDGED

> ...we shall all stand before the judgment seat of Christ.
>
> (Romans 14:10)
>
> And I saw the dead, small and great, stand before God; and the books were opened...
>
> (Revelation 20:12)

5. ALL SHALL BOW

> ...at the name of Jesus every knee should bow...
>
> (Philippians 2:10)

Right now, in simple faith, you can have the wonderful assurance of eternal life.

Ask yourself, honestly, the question...

WHAT WILL I DO WITH JESUS?

Will you accept Jesus Christ as your personal Saviour and Lord or will you reject Him?

This you must decide yourself. No one else can decide that for you. The basis of your decision should be made on God's Word—the Bible.

Jesus tells us the following:

> "...him that cometh to me I will in no wise cast out...
>
> Verily, verily I say unto you, He that believeth on me hath everlasting life"
>
> (John 6:37,47)

He also is a righteous God and a God of indignation to those who reject Him....

> "...he that believeth not is condemned already, because he hath not believed in the name of the only begotten Son of God".
>
> (John 3:18)

> "And whosoever was not found written in the book of life was cast into the lake of fire".
>
> (Revelation 20:15)

YOUR MOST IMPORTANT DECISION IN LIFE

Because sin entered the world and because God hates sin, God sent His Son Jesus Christ to die on the cross to pay the price for your sins and mine.

If you place your trust in Him, God will freely forgive you of your sins.

> "For by grace are ye saved through faith; and that not of yourselves: it is the gift of God:
>
> Not of works, lest any man should boast".
>
> (Ephesians 2:8,9)

> "...He that heareth my word, and believeth on Him that sent me, hath everlasting life, and shall not come into condemnation: but is passed from death unto life."
>
> (John 5:24)

What about you? Have you accepted Christ as your personal Saviour?

Do you realize that right now you can know the reality of this new life in Christ Jesus. Right now you can dispel the doubt that is in your mind concerning your future. Right now you can ask Christ to come into your heart. And right now you can be assured of eternal life in heaven.

All of your riches here on earth—all of your financial security—all of your material wealth, your houses, your land will crumble into nothingness in a few years.

And as God has told us:

> "As it is appointed unto men once to die, but after this the judgement:
>
> So Christ was once offered to bear the sins of many: and unto them that look for Him shall He appear the second time without sin unto salvation."
>
> (Hebrews 9:27,28)

THE CHOICE

Are you willing to sacrifice an eternity with Christ in Heaven for a few years of questionable material gain that will lead to death and destruction? If you do not accept Christ as your personal Saviour, you have only yourself to blame for the consequences.

Or would you right now, as you are reading these very words of this book, like to know without a shadow of a doubt that you are on the road to Heaven—that death is not the end of life but actually the climactic beginning of the most wonderful existence that will ever be—a life with the Lord Jesus Christ and with your friends, your relatives, and your loved ones who have accepted Christ as their Saviour.

It's not a difficult thing to do. So many religions and so many people have tried to make the simple Gospel message of Christ complex. You cannot work your way into heaven—heaven is the gift of God for those who have their sins forgiven by trusting in Jesus Christ as the one who bore their sin.

No matter how great your works—no matter how kind you are—no matter how philanthropic you are—it means nothing in the sight of God, because in the sight of God, your riches are as filthy rags.

> "...all our righteousnesses are as filthy rags...."
>
> (Isaiah 64:6)

Christ expects you to come as you are, a sinner, recognizing your need of a Saviour, the Lord Jesus Christ.

HOW TO GET TO HEAVEN

I have met many well-intentioned people who feel that "all roads lead to Heaven." This, unfortunately, is false. **All roads do NOT lead to Heaven.**

All roads lead to DEATH...except ONE ROAD and ONE WAY. Jesus Christ said:

> I am the door; by me if any man enter in, he shall be saved...
>
> *(John 10:9)*
>
> He that entereth not by the door into the sheepfold, but climbeth up some other way, the same is a thief and a robber.
>
> *(John 10:1)*
>
> Thomas saith unto Him, Lord...how can we know the way?
>
> Jesus saith unto him, I am the way, the truth and the life: no man cometh unto the Father, but by me.
>
> *(John 14:5-6)*
>
> Take heed lest any man deceive you: For many shall come in my name, saying, I am Christ; and shall deceive many.
>
> *(Mark 13:5-6)*
>
> Neither is there salvation in any other; for there is no other name under Heaven given among men, whereby we must be saved.
>
> *(Acts 4:12)*

Many people feel they will get to Heaven through the teachings of Bahai, British-Israelism (Armstrong), Buddhism, Christian Science, Jehovah's Witnesses, Mormonism or some of the mystic cults of India or Japan. **But all these roads will lead you directly to Hell!**

There are not many Teachers. There is ONE Teacher, the Lord, Christ Jesus! There are not many roads. There is ONE ROAD...the Lord, Christ Jesus. The Bible warns us:

> But though we, or an angel from Heaven, preach any other gospel unto you than that which we have preached unto you, let him be accursed.

As we said before, so say I now again, If any man preach any other gospel unto you than that ye have received, let him be accursed.

(Galatians 1:8-9)

Understanding this, why not bow your head right now and give this simple prayer of faith to the Lord.

Say it in your own words. It does not have to be a beautiful oratorical prayer—simply a prayer of humble contrition.

My Personal Decision for Christ

"Lord Jesus, I know that I'm a sinner and that I cannot save myself by good works. I believe that you died for me and that you shed your blood for my sins. I believe that you rose again from the dead. And now I am receiving you as my Messiah and personal Saviour, my Lord, my only hope of salvation and eternal life. I know that I'm a sinner and deserve to be condemned at the judgment. I know that I cannot save myself. Lord, be merciful to me, a sinner, and save me according to the promise of Your Word. I want Christ to come into my heart now to be my Saviour, Lord and Master."

Signed ....

Date ....

If you have signed the above, having just taken Christ as your personal Saviour and Lord...I would like to rejoice with you in your new found faith.

Write to me...Salem Kirban, Kent Road, Huntingdon Valley, Penna. 19006...and I'll send you a little booklet to help you start living your new life in Christ.

What is the Rapture?

This refers to the time, prior to the start of the 7 year Tribulation Period, when believing Christians (both dead and alive) will "in the twinkling of an eye" be caught up ("raptured") to meet Christ in the air.

When will it Occur?

The Bible says in Matthew 24:34, "...This generation shall not pass, till all these things be fulfilled." To some, the start of this Timetable of Events prior to the Rapture began May 14, 1948 when Israel became a nation. Since a generation is about 30 to 33 years, they say, the Rapture will occur between 1978 to 1981. Others feel that the start of Israel should begin at the 6-Day War in June, 1967 when Jerusalem became a part of Israel. Both views, however, are speculative, arriving at conclusions based on personal opinions, rather than on clear Bible teaching.

Matthew 24:34, Mark 13:28-31 and Luke 21:29-33 and Luke 21:24 may well indicate that the Rapture Countdown begins when the time of the Gentiles ends. Whether a countdown can be considered as starting in 1948 or 1967 or some other date is a matter of opinion. Even, however, if 1948 were an acceptable date...one cannot use the phrase of Matthew 24:34 "This generation..." and state that this means 30 or 33 years. This verse rather teaches that... those living in that time will not die until they see these things come to a final consummation. Thus, if someone were 1 year old in 1948, conceivably...he would see the fulfillment of the Rapture in his lifetime (and that's the key phrase)...and this could be some 70 or 80 years later. IF WE ARE in the Rapture Countdown the events will progress like lightening.

1948   Israel becomes a nation.
1967   Jerusalem at last again belongs to Israel.
1973   Nations the world over hate Israel.
19?? or 2???...How long will it be until the Messiah comes again to deliver Israel and the Earth...?

THE JUDGMENTS OF THE TRIBULATION PERIOD

	First Seal	Second Seal	Third Seal	Fourth Seal	Fifth Seal	Sixth Seal	Seventh Seal
The Seven Seal Judgments After The Rapture comes … 	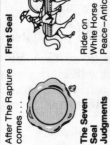 Rider on White Horse Peace—Antichrist	Rider on Red Horse War	Rider on Black Horse Famine	Rider on Pale Horse Death	Martyred Souls Persecution	Changes on Earth Destruction	Silence
The Seven Trumpet Judgments From out of the Seventh Seal comes …	 1/3 Earth afire 1/3 Trees burned All grass burned	Meteor destroys 1/3 ships, fish—1/3 sea—blood filled	Falling Star poisons 1/3 of all water	1/3 of sun, moon and stars darkened	5 months of torture by Scorpion stings	Satan's 200 million army kills 1/3 Mankind	Earthquake 7000 die in Jerusalem
The Seven Vial Judgments From out of the Seventh Trumpet comes…	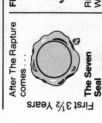 Boils affect those with Mark of Antichrist	Sea of Blood Everything in ocean dies	Rivers of Blood Rivers, springs turn to blood	Heat from Sun scorches all Mankind	Darkness Earth plunged into darkness	River Euphrates Dried up—Army attacks Israel	Hail Cities crumble

First 3½ Years / Last 3½ Years

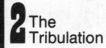

What is the Tribulation?

This is the term commonly given to the period also known as "Daniel's 70th Week" of years (Daniel 9:27). Precisely speaking, however, the Biblical period denoted by Jesus as that characterized by "Great Tribulation" is the last half of this 7 years — from the Antichrist's committing the horrible Temple desecration called "the Abomination of Desolation" to Christ's coming to destroy the armies of Antichrist gathered in the Armageddon Valley (Esdraelon-Jezreel) of Israel.

This seven years will be a period of phenomenal world trial and suffering. It is at this time that Antichrist will reign over a federation of 10 nations which quite possibly could include the United States. See Daniel 9:27 and Matthew 24:15,21.

When will it Occur?

Although no one knows the exact time that it will begin, many Scriptural promises cause us to believe that it will follow the Rapture. Whether it begins the very minute after the Rapture or several years after the Rapture we do not know. It should, however, begin in a time span soon after the Rapture. It will last 7 years.

What will Happen?

There will be 21 judgments, divided into 3 units of 7 judgments each — the 7 Seals, the 7 Trumpets, and finally the 7 Bowls of God's wrath. The first of these series of judgments are the **Seven Seal Judgments.** Christ allows a man to appear on earth who will pose as the "Saviour of the World." He will be Antichrist. War, famine, death, persecution and catastrophic changes on earth will mark these judgments. Antichrist will pretend to be a friend of Israel. After 3½ years, however, he will turn on them and persecute them severely.

What is Armageddon?

Armageddon — a strange sounding name — will be the battle ground for the greatest blood bath that the world has ever seen.

Where is Armageddon located?

Armageddon (Hebrew for: "Mount Megiddo") represents a strategic valley in Northern Israel named for the nearby ancient city of Megiddo. This city built upon a hill, Mt. Megiddo, commands the Jezreel Valley and the Plain of Esdraelon. This is the gateway through the mountains from the North to Jerusalem.

When will the Battle of Armageddon occur?

It will occur at the **end** of the 7-year Tribulation Period.

How will events bring about this Battle?

During the Tribulation Period the war machine of Russian Communism will be destroyed (Ezekiel 38:1-39:16). Two world leaders will emerge. The 10-nation European Federation will elect a powerful, personable man to lead them. He will be able to bring peace in the Middle East. He will be the **Antichrist.** A religious leader will direct all worship only to the Antichrist. He will be the **False Prophet.**

Antichrist will persecute Israel, and his power will become worldwide. China and her allies, called the "Kings of the East" in Revelation 16:12, will bring an army of 200 million towards Israel with the intent of destroying Jerusalem and taking over world leadership. Antichrist, for some diabolical cause, also causes armies from all over the earth to invade Israel. Perhaps Antichrist seeks to fight the Asian alliance. Suddenly, against both the armies of Antichrist and the armies of the East, something unusual happens. The Heavens open. Jesus Christ appears on a white horse with the armies of heaven, and destroys all these armies gathered in central Israel. More than 200 million die! The blood bath covers 185 miles of Israel! Antichrist and the False Prophet are cast into the Lake of Fire.

What is the Judgment Seat of Christ?

This is a time when believers, who have been raptured into Heaven, will stand before their Lord to receive crowns and rewards.

When will this Occur?

This will occur after the Rapture and during the Tribulation Period. The Judgement Seat of Christ will occur in Heaven (it is sometimes called "the day of Christ"). See Philippians 1:10 and 2:16. At the same time there will begin on earth what is called "the day of the Lord." This is the Tribulation Period.

Is this different than the Great White Throne Judgment?

YES! The Judgment Seat of Christ occurs immediately after the Rapture and is for believers. Believers will receive rewards. Whereas the Great White Throne Judgment is for unbelievers. This latter judgment will destine unbelievers to an eternity in Hell.

What happens at The Judgment Seat of Christ?

Each believer will appear before the judgment seat of Christ (2 Corinthians 5:10). No question of divine or eternal penalty will be raised. The believer's works will be examined. Rewards will be given based on the Lord's estimate of their value. See 1 Corinthians 3:10—4:5. Not only will our works be examined but also how well we have done these works and for what motives. The entire depth of our spiritual life, while on earth, will come up for review. If we were "surface Christians" who attended church on Sunday and were active in all types of social church activity...our rewards will be very limited. Our works have no value if they are not built on Christ. Five different crown rewards will be given. Each person will receive rewards in relation to their individual service while on earth. 1 Corinthians 3:8.

What is the Marriage of the Lamb?

It is that moment when the church (believers) is united with Christ in Heaven.

When does it Occur?

The Marriage of the Lamb occurs <u>after</u> the Rapture and <u>after</u> the Judgment Seat of Christ. It occurs in Heaven.

What Happens?

This marks a time when Christ, the heavenly bridegroom, forever will be with His beloved Church (believers). The Bride is the Church, and the Church is all the redeemed of Jesus Christ.

There will be two principals at the Marriage of the Lamb:

The Heavenly Bridegroom: Jesus Christ

The Bride: The Church, which is all the redeemed of Jesus Christ to the moment of the Rapture.

There will be great rejoicing as this long awaited true marriage between Jesus Christ and the Church is fulfilled ...a union that will last through eternity.

Will there be a Marriage Supper?

YES! Every marriage has its feast filled with joy and happiness...where everyone fellowships around a table laden with food. At this banquet of banquets will come the prophets, the Old Testament patriarchs and all the redeemed. You may be sitting next to Moses or Nehemiah or Paul or Timothy!

What will Happen Then?

After the marriage feast Christ will present His Church to the earth to reign in the 1000 year Millennium.

What is the Judgment of the Nation Israel?

This is a time when all **living** people of Jewish heritage will be judged.

When does this judgment of living Israel occur?

This occurs <u>after</u> the Battle of Armageddon and <u>before</u> the 1000 Year Millennium.

Where does it occur?

The place of judgment will be on earth. All **living** Israel will be regathered, possibly at Kadesh-Barnea or at a similar location. Kadesh-Barnea is about 65 miles south of Gaza in the Negev desert. It was here that the Israelites spent many years after their exodus from Egypt. When the Israelites reached this place, Moses sent 12 spies to scout southern Canaan. Encouraged by the Lord to invade Canaan, the Israelites rebelled. See Deuteronomy 9:23. God judged them by not permitting the rebels to enter the Promised Land.

Thus, the area of Kadesh-Barnea quite possibly, based on Ezekiel 20:34-38, could be the area where all living Jews from the four corners of the earth will be regathered.

What will happen there?

Malachi 3:2-5 speaks of the Lord's judgment being as a refiner's fire that will purify and purge living Israel. God will judge each individual separating the saved from the unsaved.

The unsaved will be cut-off and cast into Hell (Ezekiel 20:37 and Matthew 25:30).

The saved of living Israel will be taken into the 1000 year Millennium, will be resettled into Jerusalem and the Promised Land, and will reign with the Lord Jesus Christ forever.

What is the Judgment of the Gentiles?

This is a time when all **living** Gentiles who have survived the 7 year Tribulation Period will be judged. See Matthew 25:31-46.

When does this judgment occur?

This occurs <u>after</u> the Battle of Armageddon and <u>before</u> the 1000 year Millennium.

Where does it occur?

The Old Testament pictures in Joel 3:2 that God's Armageddon judgments will take place in the Valley of Jehoshaphat. The exact boundaries of this location cannot be determined. We do know that when the Lord returns to the Mount of Olives at the end of the Battle of Armageddon, a great valley will be opened (Zechariah 14:4). Jehoshaphat means "Jehovah judges." This newly opened valley, symbolic of God's judgment could be the area where the Gentiles are judged.

What will happen there?

The **living** Gentiles at this judgment who showed by their sinful lives that they had rejected the message of Christ's witnesses during the Tribulation Period will go to Hell (Matthew 25:41). Those who showed by their righteous lives that they had accepted Christ during this Period will live on earth for the Millennium Period, and then they will enter the New Heavens and New Earth.

The saved who have accepted Christ up to the point of the Rapture become **Resurrected** Believers...along with the resurrected martyrs of the Tribulation Period. Those who accept Christ after the Rapture in the 7 year Tribulation period and who survive the Tribulation alive are **Living** Believers who live on **Earth** during the Millennium prior to receiving their eternal bodies.

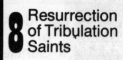

Why this additional resurrection?

Before the Tribulation Period of 7 years begins, the Rapture occurs. At this point all the Saints, living and dead...are caught up to be with Christ.

When the Tribulation Period begins many people on earth will refuse to accept the Mark of Antichrist. They will refuse to pay homage to him. In fact they will become Christians and will unashamedly testify to others about the redeeming blood of Jesus Christ. Because of their testimony, many will be beheaded. See Revelation 20:4,5.

Thus, this additional resurrection so the Tribulation Saints can join the Raptured Saints.

What about the Old Testament Saints?

The Bible does not reveal every detail of God's Plan for the future. And because of this Biblical scholars differ on exactly when the Old Testament Saints will be resurrected. Some say they will be resurrected at the Rapture...**prior** to the Tribulation Period. Others say the Old Testament Saints will be resurrected **after** the Tribulation Period **with** the Tribulation Saints. In either case, they will participate in the Marriage of Lamb...since this event continues on up to the Millennium. Daniel 12:2, Isaiah 26:19 and John 5:28,29 are good references here.

Then how many resurrections are there?

The Bible speaks of two great resurrections, the First and the Second. The one is unto life and the other is unto judgment. The First Resurrection, however, has at least two parts.

First. (a) The resurrection of believers at the Rapture
(1 Thessalonians 4:16; 1 Corinthians 15:51-53)

(b) The resurrection of Tribulation Saints
(Revelation 20:4,5)

Second. The resurrection of the unsaved at the Great White Throne Judgment
(Revelation 20:5, 11-14)

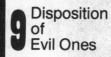
Who are the Evil Ones?

They are the three major leaders during the Tribulation Period...Antichrist and his associate, The False Prophet, and, of course, Satan. This is the False Trinity which will fully manifest itself during the end of this age.

When does judgment fall on them?

At the _end_ of the 7 year Tribulation Period.

What actually happens?

Jesus Christ, after destroying the armies of the world at the battle of Armageddon...then turns to take care of the leaders of this evil plan.

Antichrist, whose 42 months of world power began when he desecrated the Temple in Jerusalem in the middle of the 7 year Tribulation Period, now must face the consequences of his sins. He is cast into the Lake of Fire (Rev. 19:20).

The False Prophet, a religious leader, who directed allegiance to Antichrist, is also cast into the Lake of Fire (Revelation 19:20).

They are not merely slain...as the multitudes are who took part in the Battle of Armageddon. Both of these masterminds of iniquity are actually cast **alive** into the Lake of Fire without waiting for any final judgment.

What is the Lake of Fire?

It is the place of eternal suffering burning with brimstone, a place of perpetual darkness with no hope of deliverance.

What happens to Satan?

Satan at this time is bound in the bottomless pit for 1000 years. He does not reappear until the end of the Millennium Period. The bottomless pit is not necessarily Hades or Hell but a holding place where Satan is bound in chains (Revelation 20:1-3).

What is the Millennium?

This is a period when earth again is placed under the direct rule of God, and when all the believers of all the ages reign with Christ. It is not yet, however, the perfect state of the New Earth and the New Heavens which comes later.

Those previously resurrected at the Rapture and those saints who died in the Tribulation and were resurrected along with Old Testament saints...will reign with Christ in the Millennial Age as **Resurrected Believers.** This includes all of the believers who, alive at the time of the Rapture, were then changed "in the twinkling of an eye."

When will this occur?

The Millennium will occur **after** the Tribulation Period.

Are there two types of Believers at that time?

YES. There are **Resurrected Believers** and **Living Believers.** **Resurrected Believers**, those already raised from the dead, have been previously described above. They will be given positions of responsibility in the Millennial Kingdom (Matthew 19:28, Luke 19: 12-27).

Living Believers will be Gentiles and Jews alike who are still living at the close of Armageddon, and who are permitted to enter the Millennial Kingdom. These were not raptured (they were not believers at the time of the Rapture), nor did they die in the Tribulation Period (they survived). They are still in their human unresurrected bodies.

Will Living Believers still have children?

YES. During the Millennium these **Living Believers** will still be fully normal people who are able to reproduce children. Children born of these Living Believers will still be born with a sin nature. And for them, as for all humans born at any time, salvation is still required. They must individually make a decision whether to accept Jesus Christ as Saviour and Lord...or to deny Him.

What is the Final Rebellion?

This is a time when Satan will have a brief and last opportunity to deceive people.

When does this occur?

This will happen at the **end** of the 1000 year Period.

How can Satan get a following after 1000 years of peace and happiness?

You must remember that many will be born during this 1000 years. And, as ideal as the Millennium will be it still will not be Heaven. Many born during this 1000 years will not become believers. Sin will still be possible. Although the majority of those born during the Millennium will no doubt follow Christ, yet other multitudes will not believe. Some will refuse to go up to Jerusalem to worship the Lord (Zechariah 14:17-19). Christ rules with an "iron rod" in a theocratic government during this Millennial reign. Because of this some will inwardly rebel. Once and for all, God will give them this last opportunity to voluntarily choose between His Kingdom or Satan's. Like Adam and Eve, they will be given an opportunity to choose life or death.

How many decide to follow Satan?

The Bible says in Revelation 20:7,8 "...Satan shall be loosed out of his prison...to gather them (the unbelievers) together to battle: the number of whom is as the sand of the sea." This could involve millions of people.

What is the outcome of this revolt?

This vast number of people will completely encircle the Living Believers within the capital city, Jerusalem, in a state of siege. When this occurs, God brings fire down from Heaven killing the millions of Satan's army (Revelation 20). Satan is then cast into the Lake of Fire where Antichrist and The False Prophet already are.

What is the Great White Throne Judgment?

This is the final judgment of the unsaved, non-believers, of **all** of the ages. These are resurrected for this event and they are judged before God.

When does this Judgment occur?

This occurs **after** the Final Rebellion at the end of the Millennial Period.

What actually happens?

Immediately prior to this, at the close of the Millennium, as we have seen, Satan was cast into the Lake of Fire where the Antichrist and the False Prophet have already been for 1000 years.

Now, before the Great White Throne are arraigned all of the unrepentant sinners of the ages. This throne is different from the throne of the Tribulation Period. That throne had a rainbow around it (Revelation 4:3) indicating God would show mercy and many would be saved during the Tribulation Period (Revelation 7).

But the Great White Throne has **no rainbow.** No more mercy will be extended. The God of love is now a God of JUDGMENT. The whiteness of the throne stands for God's unspotted holiness. This holiness condemns all of the unrepentant sinners of all of the ages.

Not only do the living unbelievers face this judgment but all the lost dead of all the ages are raised from the dead to face this same judgment. Here is the saddest roll call in history! No matter how rich you are in today's world... money does not buy your way into Heaven...no more than good works!

All these unbelievers are then cast in the Lake of Fire (Revelation 20:15). Thus ends...and begins...the most tragic moment in history...a moment that for the unbeliever will begin an eternity in constant torment and eternal separation from God, called in the Bible, "the Second Death" (Revelation 20:14).

When does this present Earth burn up?

This present earth is purified **after** the Final rebellion which closes the Millennium of 1000 years.

Why is the earth destroyed?

It is **not** really destroyed. It is purified through burning. Because the earth has become so polluted with sin, God desires to wipe the slate entirely clean from every trace of that sin. He will do this by purging the earth by fire... giving His Saints a New Heaven and a New Earth.

What does occur?

In the New Testament 2 Peter 3:3-12 we are told five important facts:

1. This event will occur SUDDENLY
2. The Heavens will pass away WITH A GREAT NOISE
3. The Elements will melt with a FERVENT HEAT
4. The Earth will be BURNED UP
5. Everything on the Earth will be BURNED UP

The Sun, 100 times the diameter of the earth, has the capacity to generate a heat so intense it could set the entire earth afire. If you could build a cake of ice 1½ miles square and 93 million miles high...it would reach from earth to sun. Scientists tell us, if the full power of the sun were focused on this cake of ice it would be completely melted in just 30 seconds!

In this, God's final judgment, the intensive fire will melt all the elements of the earth, burn the earth, set the atmospheric heavens on fire and in that fire...dissolve those heavens! Some have suggested that this final fire of purification when "the elements shall melt with fervent heat" will be a divinely originated nuclear inferno — refining by fire the former sin cursed planet (2 Peter 3:10).

When do the New Heavens and New Earth become a reality?

The New Heavens and the New Earth will be formed after this present Earth burns up and is purified. This is the **LAST** and final part of God's eternal plan for mankind.

Who will be in the New Heavens and the New Earth?

All the Old Testament saints, all the New Testament saints, and all of the Tribulation and Millennial saints. In other words all the redeemed (saved) of all the ages will be there! This will be the ultimate in glory reigning forever with Christ in a New Heaven and a New Earth (Revelation 21).

How will the New Earth be different from this present Earth?

1. Every believer will have a NEW BODY.
   It will be an imperishable body. No longer will we be plagued with illness or death; nor will there be any tears in Heaven but rather, eternal joy!
2. There will be NO NIGHT.
   Christ will be the light that illumines all.
3. There will be NO MORE SEPARATION.
   All our loved ones who are believers will be there.
4. There will be NO HUNGER NOR FAMINE.
   The Tree of Life will provide sufficient for all.

Where will the New City of Jerusalem be?

The New City, JERUSALEM, will not be identical in size or boundaries to the city on this present earth that we know today as Jerusalem. The New Jerusalem will be approximately 1500 miles on each side and could conceivably hold according to some theoretical calculations 53 billion people. Revelation 21:1-22:5 gives the most extensive revelation of the eternal home of the redeemed. Will you be there?